Psychology:
A New Introduction

for AS Level

Teacher's Guide

Geoff Rolls
Judith Munro
Alex Banks
and
James Larcombe

Hodder & Stoughton

A MEMBER OF THE HODDER HEADLINE GROUP

Acknowledgements

The publishers would like to thank The Times Newpapers Ltd for permission to reproduce the articles appearing on pages 47 and 103, and their authors Jeremy Laurance, and Nick Nuttall and Nigel Hawkes respectively.

Artwork on page 65 by Sally Michel.

Orders: please contact Bookpoint Ltd, 130 Milton Park, Abingdon, Oxon OX14 4SB.
Telephone: (44) 01235 827720. Fax: (44) 01235 400454. Lines are open from 9.00–6.00, Monday to Saturday, with a 24 hour message answering service. Email address: orders@bookpoint.co.uk

British Library Cataloguing in Publication Data
A catalogue record for this title is available from the British Library

ISBN 0 340 80386 X

First Published 2001

Impression number   10 9 8 7 6 5 4 3 2 1

Year   2007 2006 2005 2004 2003 2002 2001

Typeset by GreenGate Publishing Services, Tonbridge, Kent.

Printed in Great Britain for Hodder & Stoughton Educational, a division of Hodder Headline Plc, 338 Euston Road, London NW1 3BH by Hobbs The Printers Ltd.

Contents

How to use this book

This book is written to accompany *Psychology: A New Introduction for A Level* by Gross, McIlveen *et al.* (2000). It contains activities based on the AQA AS psychology specification, but many of the activities are relevant to other specifications. Page references throughout refer to the full A level text; for students using the AS book you will need to subtract eight pages to obtain the correct page number.

One of the most challenging facets of teaching is to engage the student in an interactive learning experience. As psychologists, we know that students learn best by 'doing' rather than merely listening. Indeed, it is sometimes said that you remember 20 per cent of what you are told and 90 per cent of what you do. However, preparing 'active' materials for use in this way can take a considerable amount of time and effort. The activities contained in this book help to address this, with numerous small group or individual activities designed to be stimulating, interesting and educative.

Each chapter relates to a module within the AQA AS Specification A. Students should not be expected to complete all of the activities within their course; indeed, time would almost certainly not allow this. However, all of the activities are directly related to a specific sub-section within each module and so it is envisaged that a teacher will choose those activities that fit in best with their own teaching schedule. The activities vary in style, presentation and planning from the very straightforward, simple activity to more complex, challenging ones. Again, it is envisaged that teachers will choose those activities they feel will be most suitable for their students.

Each activity follows a similar format, with an objective outlined, a short introduction, materials listed and details of how to carry out the specific activity. There is also a suggested homework assignment. Activities have been kept on separate pages so that the teacher can photocopy the whole page onto an overhead transparency to help minimise lesson preparation time.

Wherever possible website references have been included for activities. However, due to the everchanging nature of the internet, it is worth checking that the site recommended still exists and still contains the relevant information before you commence with the task.

We hope that you enjoy conducting the activities and would welcome feedback on any of them or suggestions for further activities.

Geoff Rolls
Judith Munro
Alex Banks
James Larcombe

1 *Cognitive Psychology: Human Memory*

Specification topic	Gross, McIlveen et al., (2000) 2nd edition	Activity	Page
Short term and long term memory	**18–28**		
• Nature and structure of memory	19–22	1 Testing the capacity of STM 2 Improving STM 3 Is coding in STM acoustic? 4 Acoustic or semantic coding in STM?	2 3 4 5
• Multi-store model of memory (Atkinson and Shiffrin)	22–23	5 Does LTM affect STM capacity? 6 The serial position curve 7 The two way flow of information between STM and LTM	7 8 11
• Working memory (Baddeley and Hitch)	23–25	8 Support for the working memory model?	13
• Levels of processing (Craik and Lockhart)	25–27	9 Evidence for the levels of processing model? 10 Evidence against the levels of processing model?	15 18
Forgetting	**29–35**		
• Forgetting in STM (decay and displacement)	29–30		

• Forgetting in LTM (retrieval failure and interference)	31–33	11 Interference as an explanation for forgetting in LTM?
		12 Does retrieval-failure theory explain aspects of forgetting?
		  a Where is that memory?
		  b Do category cues help memory recall?
			19
			21
			22
			23

• Emotional factors in forgetting (flashbulb memory and repression)	33–35	13 Recalling 'flashbulb' memories	25
• Critical issue Eye witness testimony (Loftus)	36–43	14 The effect of leading questions on EWT	26
• Reconstructive memory	36–41	15 The 'War of the Ghosts' serial reproduction task 16 How schemata affect our memory	28 29
• Face recognition	41–42		
• Additional work	–	17 Memory spidergram	30
		18 Revision summary: Memory	31
		19 Revision exercise	32
		20 Multiple choice questions	33

General textbooks

1 **Gross, R. & McIlveen, R.** (1998) *Psychology: A New Introduction.* (1st edition) Hodder & Stoughton.

2 **Gross, R. & McIlveen, R.** *et al.* (2000) *Psychology: A New Introduction.* (2nd edition) Hodder & Stoughton

3 **Gross, R.** (2001) *Psychology: The Science of Mind and Behaviour.* (4th edition) Hodder & Stoughton

Activity 1 Testing the capacity of STM

Objective

To investigate the capacity of short term memory (STM) using the 'digit span' technique.

Introduction

Short term memory is the system for storing and retrieving information over a brief period of time (usually judged to be less than 30 seconds). Testing the capacity of STM dates back to 1887 when a London schoolteacher, Mr J Jacobs, devised a technique for testing STM capacity called 'the digit span'.

HOW DO YOU DO IT?

This is a very simple procedure. You need to write out rows of random numbers, gradually increasing the row lengths up to a maximum of ten numbers. For example:

3224
2765
63178
38794
679547
etc.

Read your lists out slowly to a partner in as monotonous a fashion as possible. After each row, your partner must repeat the numbers back in the correct order (you may have to get participants to read the lists and then write them down to prevent interference from other participants nearby!) When they no longer consistently recall the sequence correctly make a note of the number of digits they could recall. This is an approximate measure of their STM. The most common score is about six or seven digits – anywhere in the range five to nine would not be unexpected.

- Make brief notes on the aim, method and results of this study. Try to evaluate the study in as much detail as possible.

Notes

Miller (1956) claimed STM was limited to 7 ± 2 ('*the magic seven*'). You can read the original paper by Miller on the following website (warning: it is complicated!):
http://psychclassics.yorku.ca/Miller/
The York University, Toronto, website has a wealth of psychology-related information.

Homework (and website references)

Test your sensory memory by accessing the website:
http://coglab.psych.purdue.educoglab/Labs/PartialReport.html
Be prepared to report your findings and results to the class next lesson.

Essential reading

Gross, McIlveen *et al.* (2000) pages 19–21 to consolidate your learning.

Activity 2 Improving STM capacity

Objective

To demonstrate that STM can be improved through 'chunking'.

Introduction

One way to improve STM would be to speak the numbers aloud (assuming you didn't do this before). Another way is to group the digits together into groups of three and say them aloud, rhythmically. Grouping digits together is called 'chunking' and is a well known mnemonic or memory aid. People often do this with telephone numbers to aid recall. Notice that British telephone numbers tend to be six digits long (excluding area codes) and are therefore designed to be within most people's STM capacity.

HOW DO YOU DO IT?

Repeat the procedure from Activity 1, but this time 'chunk' the numbers into groups of two, three and four.

- Report back to the class how many numbers ('bits' of information) could be reported using these procedures.
- Does the chunk size matter?
- What does this add to our understanding of the capacity of STM?

Notes

Although each chunk (rule) can generate a large amount of information, the number of chunks is still limited to 7 ± 2.

Website reference

Sternberg (1966) developed a memory search technique which showed how information is retrieved in STM. You can try his experiment at:
http://coglab.psych.purdue.educoglab/Labs/Sternberg.html
Be prepared to report your findings and results to the class next lesson.

Activity 3 Is coding in STM acoustic?

Objective

To discover whether information is encoded in STM on an acoustic basis.

Introduction

There are many differences between STM and LTM. These mainly apply to the capacity, duration and coding of the memories in the different stores. This activity tests the nature of STM coding and is a simple adaptation of Conrad (1964) who tested 387 participants!

HOW DO YOU DO IT?

You need to make two ten letter lists. One list must comprise letters which sound similar, the other letters that sound different. For example:

List A: C D G T P V E B G (list of letters sound similar)
List B: N W A X Q Z L K R (list of letters that sound different)

Read out list A to your participants. They must write down their recall of the given list immediately afterwards (in order to test STM). Repeat this procedure with list B.

- Compare the scores from list A with those from list B.
- Did the participants make any mistakes in their recall and if so, what were they?
- Explain your findings in terms of STM coding and storage.
- What methodological difficulties were encountered with this design?
- What kind of experimental design was employed here?
- How could the experiment have been improved? (Include the terms 'counterbalancing' and 'order effects' in your answer.)

Notes

- You could repeat the experiment but this time ask the participants to *read* rather than *listen* to the two lists. The information would still be stored in STM but the initial *processing* of the information would be different. Results are likely to be similar, which emphasises the way most information is stored in STM regardless of the way in which it was initially coded.
- It is wrong to imply that all STM is coded acoustically. STM can code some semantic and visual information (see Activity 5 and Activity 6).

Homework

Summarise the main differences between STM and LTM and describe two studies which highlight these differences (maximum 200 words).

Essential reading

Gross, McIlveen *et al.* (2000), page 22.

Website reference

http://coglab.psych.purdue.educoglab/Labs/MemorySpan.html
Access this site and enter as 'guest' in the user ID text file. Click on next trial to start.

A *ctivity 4* Acoustic or semantic coding in STM?

Objective

To test whether STM coding favours acoustic or semantic coding.

Introduction

This is similar to Activity 3 except that it involves words instead of letters. It might be argued that because of this it has greater ecological validity. The use of words ensures that material will be encoded on a semantic and acoustic basis. It is an adaptation of a study reported by Baddeley (1966). It is worth carrying out the variation listed in the notes below involving delayed memory recall where LTM is tested.

HOW DO YOU DO IT?

Using the word lists below, you need to start with List A followed by B, C and D.
Read (at normal reading speed) the first column of five words in List A and then cover the list and try to write them down on a separate piece of paper. They must be written in the correct sequence to count as correct. Move on to the next column and repeat the procedure outlined for each of the five columns per list. Repeat this procedure for all four word lists.

List A

mad	mat	can	map	cap
cap	can	cat	cad	map
cat	map	map	man	mat
map	mad	man	mad	man
cad	cat	cap	can	can

List B

pen	few	cup	day	cow
cow	cup	day	cup	pit
bar	cow	bar	few	few
day	pit	pit	pen	hot
cup	hot	few	pit	bar

List C

big	long	tall	broad	wide
wide	tall	broad	tall	large
high	wide	high	long	long
broad	large	large	big	great
tall	great	long	large	high

List D

foul	late	thin	old	strong
strong	thin	hot	deep	old
hot	old	late	safe	late
old	foul	safe	foul	safe
deep	hot	strong	thin	thin

As you will have noticed, list A has acoustically similar words in it.
List B is composed of equally common words to those in list A but they sound different to each other.
List C is composed of adjectives with similar meanings.
List D is composed of adjectives with different meanings to one another.

- For each list multiply the total number of words you recalled in the correct order by four to get a percentage figure for each list.
- Plot this percentage figure on an appropriate chart, with lists A, B, C and D on the x axis and the percentage of correctly recalled words on the y axis.
- What do the results show? Explain your answer in terms of your knowledge of STM coding.

Notes

- Baddeley (1966) reported that the percentages of correctly recalled five sequence words for each list (i.e. you had to recall all the words in each column to count as correct) were approximately:
    10 per cent for List A
    82 per cent for List B
    65 per cent for List C
    71 per cent for List D.

- You could repeat the experiment but delay recall (i.e. test LTM). How do you think the results would change?

Website reference

http://olias.arc.nasa.gov/cognition/tutorials/STM/index.html
This is an excellent experiment which demonstrates how memorable different stimulus materials (words, images or sounds) are in STM. The expectation is that acoustic processing is best for STM. You need a PC with sound for this site.

Activity 5 Does LTM affect STM capacity?

Objective

To see if LTM interacts with STM capacity or whether LTM and STM are separate, distinct systems.

Introduction

This study will demonstrate the effects of 'chunking' on STM using letters rather than numbers but it will also demonstrate a link between STM and LTM and as such, it provides a link onto the topic of LTM. The activity outlined below is a simple adaptation of the Bower & Springston (1970) study.

HOW DO YOU DO IT?

Copy out list A shown below, and ask half your participants to read the letters and then recall them in any order (a free recall task).

List A: fbiciaibmitvpcphdbbc

With the remaining participants, repeat the procedure using list B.

List B: fbi cia ibm itv pc phd bbc

'Pool' the data collected from the class and compare the results for each group.

- Using the data collected from this exercise, draw a chart or graph which best illustrates the data collected from this exercise. (Read Gross, McIlveen *et al.* (2000), pages 166–168 for help with this)
- What explanations might account for such findings?
- In your answer consider methodological issues (such as problems of 'independent groups design') as well as theoretical considerations.

Notes

It is expected that the recall of list B would be better than that of list A because the participants have brought some meaning from their LTM to the group of letters. For example, fbi = Federal Bureau of Investigation, and so on.

Essential reading

Read Box 2.3 in Gross, McIlveen *et al.* (2000), page 20 to consolidate your learning.

Activity 6 The serial position curve

Objective

To investigate the serial position curve using a free recall technique.

Introduction

One attempt to explain how information flows from one storage system to another (STM to LTM) is Atkinson & Shiffrin's (1968, 1971) multi-store model. A key feature of this model is that STM and LTM can be viewed as two separate and distinct systems (hence the model's name). The following activity should provide evidence to support this and is a simple adaptation of Murdock's (1962) serial position curve experiment. If you have access to a PC and the Internet you can carry out this experiment at the website listed below. Alternatively, you will have to use pen and paper methods as outlined.

Materials

See page 10.

HOW DO YOU DO IT?

Devise five lists of ten commonly used words such as: desk, boy, apple, tiger, etc. Read the lists of words out loud to your participants at the approximate rate of one per second. The words must always be read in the same list order. Ask the participants to write down, in any order, as many of the words as possible (a free recall task). You need to note which words were recalled not the total number recalled. On the following page, there are some lists and a table for you to record your data, but it might be preferable if you devise your own.

- Devise a frequency table showing how many times the participants recalled each of the words on the list. Work out the percentage of correct recall of each word in the list. Was the first word on the list recalled 100 per cent of the time?
- Draw a frequency polygon of the data collected. The figure you draw is called a serial position curve.
- Look at the curve and explain your findings in terms of primacy and recency effects.
- Why are the words in the middle of the list remembered least well?
- How does this support the multi-store model?

Notes

- A variation of this study was conducted by Glanzer & Cunitz (1966) and is very easy to replicate. You need to repeat the study above but delay the participants recall by at least 30 seconds. It is suggested that you use the Brown–Peterson counting technique to do this.
- How do you think the results would change?
- Why did Glanzer and Cunitz delay recall for 30 seconds?
- Describe the Brown–Peterson technique mentioned.

Homework

Summarise the clinical studies of amnesia (such as K.F. and H.M.) which also provide evidence to support the multi-store model (maximum 100 words).

Essential reading

Read Gross, McIlveen *et al.* (2000), pages 22–23 to consolidate your learning.

Website reference

http://coglab.psych.purdue.educoglab/Labs/SerialPosition.html
At this site, you can carry out the serial position curve experiment without making up your own word lists. Type 'guest' into the user ID text file and click on start.

Activity 6 **Response sheet**

There are five word lists below. Read through each list carefully ONCE, then cover them up and write down as many words as you can recall, in any order (this is a free recall task). When you have completed all five lists, fill in the table below, ticking the appropriate boxes, that is, if you remembered the first four words and last four words in list 1, tick the boxes 1, 2, 3, 4, 12, 13, 14, and 15 in column one. You will then need to total the number of ticks for each row. This gives the total number of words recalled, corresponding to their place in the list. Transfer these totals onto the graph below.

	List 1	List 2	List 3	List 4	List 5
1	floor	desk	table	chair	clock
2	flower	tree	bush	grass	bench
3	America	Spain	Italy	Portugal	France
4	carpet	vase	video	sofa	lamp
5	laugh	smile	frown	grimace	ridicule
6	animal	voice	blood	glass	fruit
7	point	front	month	attention	guide
8	race	degree	roof	land	hand
9	hair	skin	nail	eye	meat
10	chief	boat	wife	son	daughter

Serial position of word in list	List number					Total number of words recalled
	1	2	3	4	5	
1						
2						
3						
4						
5						
6						
7						
8						
9						
10						

Frequency	5										
	4										
	3										
	2										
	1										
	0	1	2	3	4	5	6	7	8	9	10
	Serial position of word in list										

Recall of words, in serial order, from the five word lists

If the experiment has worked, you should end up with a U-shaped curve on the graph, demonstrating the primacy and recency effect (see Gross, McIlveen *et al.* (2000) Figure 2.3, page 22).

(Adapted from Baddeley, A. (1982), *Your Memory: A User's Guide*, Penguin UK)

Activity 7 The two-way flow of information between STM and LTM

Objective

To demonstrate that STM and LTM are not completely separate memory stores and that information does, in fact, flow between them.

Introduction

You will be aware of the multi-store model proposed by Atkinson & Shiffrin (1968, 1971) and evidence which has been proposed to support this model. However, there are studies which refute the clear-cut distinction between STM and LTM. These include Miller & Selfridge's (1950) experiment mentioned on page 23 of Gross, McIlveen *et al.* (2000). Another interesting study conducted by Morris *et al.* (1985) demonstrates this.

Materials

See the following page.

HOW DO YOU DO IT?

Devise a short questionnaire (15 questions) to test football knowledge. Include a range of diffi-cult and easy questions to avoid the 'ceiling' and 'floor' effect. You may wish to conduct a pilot study to check this.
Collect the football fixtures for the coming weekend and make up arbitrary scores for each of the matches.
Administer the football knowledge questionnaire and then read out your fictitious list of football results and ask your participants to recall the results. Award one mark for each team's correct score.

- Pool all the data and produce a scattergraph of your results.
- Explain your findings. Does there appear to be any correlation between knowledgeable partic-ipants and their STM recall of the fictitious results?
- Try to relate your findings to the transfer of LTM and how it can affect STM.
- Make notes on this study and emphasise how it can be used to evaluate the multi-store model.

Notes

Interest and knowledge from LTM must affect STM performance on the fictitious football scores.

Homework

Make notes on the studies by Miller & Selfridge (1950) page 20 and De Groot (1966) page 23 in Gross, McIlveen *et al.* (2000).

Essential reading

Read Gross, McIlveen *et al.* (2000), pages 20–22 to consolidate your knowledge.

Football knowledge questionnaire

1 If you had three lions on your international soccer shirt, which country would you be playing for?
2 Which European country soccer team traditionally plays in orange shirts?
3 Who scored a hat-trick in the 1966 World Cup final?
4 Who else scored for England when they last won the World Cup?
5 Who missed crucial penalties for England in the World Cup semi-final of 1990?
6 How many times have Celtic won the European Champions' Cup?
7 Who scored Manchester United's winning goal in the 1999 Champions' Cup Final win over Bayern Munich?
8 Name England's second highest goal scorer of all time.
9 What is the name of Everton's home ground?
10 Who scored twice for France in their World Cup final win in 1998?
11 Which team play at Ibrox Park?
12 In which country was the 1986 World Cup played?
13 Who beat Manchester United to win the FA Cup in 1976?
14 Why did Manchester United not win the FA Cup in 2000?
15 Which team have the nickname of the Foxes?

Total score: (maximum 15 marks)

Answers

1 England
2 Holland
3 Geoff Hurst
4 Martin Peters
5 Chris Waddle and Stuart Pearce
6 Once
7 Ole Gunnar Solksjaer
8 Gary Lineker
9 Goodison Park
10 Zinedine Zidane
11 Glasgow Rangers
12 Mexico
13 Southampton
14 They took part in the World Club Championship in Brazil instead and did not enter the FA Cup
15 Leicester City

Imaginary football results

Arsenal 1	Tottenham Hotspur 1
Aston Villa 2	Manchester United 3
Charlton 0	Manchester City 0
Chelsea 4	Bradford City 0
Derby County 1	Southampton 2
Everton 2	Liverpool 2
Ipswich 1	Leeds United 0
Middlesbrough 1	Newcastle United 2
Sunderland 4	Coventry 0

Award one mark for each team's score and one mark for remembering who was playing whom. Thus there is a maximum of three marks for each match.

Total score (Maximum = 27 marks)

Activity 8 Support for the working memory model?

Objective

To find evidence to support the working memory model.

Introduction

The working memory model was proposed by Baddeley & Hitch (1974) to explain the detail of how STM works. Instead of a single, simple STM, they proposed a more complex, multi-component 'working memory' comprising an articulatory (or phonological) loop, a visuo-spatial scratch pad, and a central executive. The activity below shows evidence for acoustic and visual processing in STM and is an adaptation of Den Heyer & Barrett (1971).

Materials

Letter grid, two pattern grids (see below) and as many blank 6 × 4 grids as there are participants.

HOW DO YOU DO IT?

You need to draw a series of grids of 24 squares (six columns by four rows). Place one letter into each of seven of the grid squares at random. For example:

Letter grid

C				K	
	Z		Y		G
	T				H

Next draw two patterned grids, each with a different pattern of seven squares coloured in. For example:

Pattern one

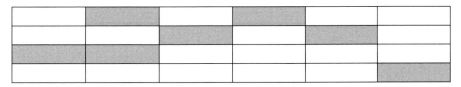

Pattern two

Next, you need to show half of the participants (Group 1) the letter grid for ten seconds and then ask them to count backwards in threes for ten seconds starting from a random three-figure number. This prevents letter rehearsal and represents the verbal task. After this, they will need to fill in a blank grid indicating where they think the letters were. If the participants remember a letter but not the square they should put it in any square, if they remember the position of the letter but not the letter, they should add any letter to that square.

The other participants (Group 2) should be shown the letter grid for ten seconds as for Group 1, but the intervening task this time involves showing them the two pattern grids above for ten seconds after which they have to tick which parts of the two grids match. This represents the visual task.

All the participants should be marked in two ways. Give them a mark out of seven for the number of correct letters they recall regardless of position on the grid (the 'letter recall score') and a mark for the number of positions they recall correctly regardless of the letter in the square (the 'position score'). If they recall all the letters in the correct position their marks would be seven and seven.

- What do the results suggest?
- Were there marked differences between Group 1 and Group 2 in their letter recall scores and position scores?
- Explain your findings in the light of your knowledge of the working memory model.

Notes

The experiment is supposed to show that the letters were encoded acoustically. This is because the verbal task affected acoustic rehearsal and therefore Group 1 should have performed worse on the letter recall. However, the position of the letters was encoded visually and therefore the intervening pattern visual task affected the position grid recall so Group 2 should have performed worse on the position score.

Homework

Describe and evaluate the working memory model (200 words maximum).

Essential reading

Read Gross, McIlveen *et al.* (2000), pages 23–25 in order to understand the working memory model.

Activity 9 Evidence for the levels of processing model?

Objective

To show gradually enhanced recall as participants process information at a progressively deeper level; an idea suggested by Craik & Lockhart (1972).

Introduction

Craik & Lockhart (1972) suggest that it is not rehearsal as such which is important for memory but what is done with the information during rehearsal. They believe that information can be processed to different depths, or levels, as the model's name implies. They suggested that there are three levels: shallow processing, phonemic processing and semantic processing. The activity below should provide support for this idea.

Materials

See the following page.

HOW DO YOU DO IT?

You need to prepare 30 questions to which participants have to answer either 'yes' or 'no'. Questions have been created on the following page but you could make up your own.
Ten of the questions will require shallow processing in which participants recognise the shape of a word. For example:

Question		Circle correct answer
Is the word in capitals?	DESK	Yes/No
Is the word in lower case?	Flower	Yes/No

Ten of the questions require more complex phonemic processing involving the sound of the word. For example:

Question		Circle correct answer
Does the word rhyme with cat?	Sky	Yes/No
Does the word rhyme with house?	Mouse	Yes/No

Ten of the questions require even more complex (!) processing involving the meaning of the word. This is called semantic processing. For example:

Question		Circle correct answer
Is the word a vegetable?	Tomato	Yes/No
Is the word the name of a country?	Sydney	Yes/No

Write out the thirty questions in a random order. Ask participants to circle the answers as quickly as they can, whilst ensuring they get the answers correct.
Take away the question paper and ask them to count backwards in threes out loud from a three digit number you specify (this is to prevent rehearsal). After 30 seconds, ask them to write down on a clean sheet of paper all the 30 words in the middle column that they have just classified.

- Draw a bar chart of the percentage of correct participant recalls for visual appearance processing, phonemic processing and semantic processing. Remember to label the graph fully.
- Explain your findings in terms of Craik & Lockhart's (1975) levels of processing model.

Notes

- Craik & Tulving (1975) found approximate recall of 10 per cent for visual condition, 15 per cent for the phonemic processing condition and 30 per cent recall for semantic processing.
- The effect is even more marked for two presentations of the classified words, particularly with respect to the semantic word recall scores (approximately 60 per cent recall).

Essential reading

Read Gross, McIlveen *et al.* (2000), pages 25–27 in order to understand the levels of processing model.

Activity 9 Response sheet

Questions for use with Activity 9

1	Is the word in lower case?	trousers	YES/NO
2	Does the word rhyme with book?	COOK	YES/NO
3	Is it the name of an animal?	Lemur	YES/NO
4	Is the word in upper case?	BUTTON	YES/NO
5	Does the word rhyme with sock?	Desk	YES/NO
6	Is it the name of a fruit?	orange	YES/NO
7	Is the word in lower case?	BOTTLE	YES/NO
8	Does the word rhyme with flare?	Chair	YES/NO
9	Is it the name of a country?	Peru	YES/NO
10	Is the word in upper case?	FOOTBALL	YES/NO
11	Does the word rhyme with bucket?	CLOCK	YES/NO
12	Is it the name of a vegetable?	chicken	YES/NO
13	Is the word in upper case?	COMPUTER	YES/NO
14	Does the word rhyme with dog?	FOG	YES/NO
15	Is it the name of an English town?	Birmingham	YES/NO
16	Is the word in lower case?	sink	YES/NO
17	Does the word rhyme with skunk?	MOUSE	YES/NO
18	Is it the name of a kitchen utensil?	chainsaw	YES/NO
19	Is the word in upper case?	TAXI	YES/NO
20	Does the word rhyme with cat?	Tights	YES/NO
21	Is it the name of a tree?	OAK	YES/NO
22	Is the word in upper case?	plug	YES/NO
23	Does the word rhyme with bar?	car	YES/NO
24	Is it the name of a colour?	BLUE	YES/NO
25	Is the word in lower case?	bike	YES/NO
26	Does the word rhyme with fork?	STORK	YES/NO
27	Is it the name of a building?	LIBRARY	YES/NO
28	Is the word in upper case?	gun	YES/NO
29	Does the word rhyme with tap?	cap	YES/NO
30	Is it the name of a mountain?	EVEREST	YES/NO

Activity 10 Evidence against the levels of processing model?

Objective

To demonstrate that it is not merely depth of processing which affects memory recall.

Introduction

The activity should provide evidence that other factors might be associated with memory recall, just beyond depth of processing. This is a simple replication of a study conducted by Tyler *et al.* (1979).

Materials

Two anagram lists shown below.

HOW DO YOU DO IT?

Ask two groups of participants to each solve one of the lists of anagrams below. You may have to give clues for list 2 if it is *too* difficult!

Anagram list 1	Anagram list 2	Answers
potaot	totaop	potato
camle	elmca	camel
glssa	aslgs	glass
biclyec	lccbeiy	bicycle
toite	ltteoi	toilet
rgass	srsga	grass
cartep	tcrepa	carpet
loonbal	olnoalb	balloon

After the participants have solved all the anagrams, ask them to recall the words they solved.

- Compare how many words were recalled from the two lists. Do your findings fit in with the levels of processing model? According to the LOP model, recall should be the same since they both involved the same semantic level of processing.
- Are there any differences in the processing required between the two lists? How difficult was each list? Which was the quickest to solve? Might these factors be involved in recall performance?
- Hopefully you have identified two variables which might explain any difference in recall scores across the two lists. These are possible 'confounding variables'; explain the term in relation to this experiment.

Notes

- It is expected that participants will have recalled more from list 2. This is surprising (according to the LOP model) since both word lists were processed to the same semantic level and therefore recall should be the same for each list.
- This activity provides evidence to suggest that processing effort, and time spent processing information, may play a part in memory recall.

Homework

Describe and evaluate the evidence for and against the levels of processing model (200 words maximum).

Essential reading

Gross, McIlveen *et al.* (2000), page 27.

Activity 11 Interference as an explanation for forgetting in LTM?

Objective

To demonstrate that interference does appear to be implicated in laboratory studies of forgetting in LTM.

Introduction

According to interference theory, forgetting is influenced more by what we do before or after learning than by the passage of time or retrieval failure. The activity outlined below is a simple adaptation of McGeoch & McDonald (1931).

Materials

Adjective lists shown below.

HOW DO YOU DO IT?

Ask participants to learn Adjective list 1 below until they can recall it perfectly.

Adjective list 1:	Adjective list 2:
Tall	Big
Blue	Green
Dull	Slow
Fast	Vivacious
Delicious	Adorable
Angelic	Cold
Wet	Poor
Late	Bright
Shiny	Funny
Beautiful	Cheerful

Ask one third of your participants (Group A) to rest quietly for ten minutes before recalling the list.

Ask one third of your participants (Group B) to learn ten three-digit numbers for ten minutes and then ask them to recall the adjectives.

Ask the remaining third of your participants (Group C) to learn Adjective list 2 for ten minutes and then ask them to recall list 1.

- Draw a summary table of the results, showing the mean recall of the ten adjectives.
- What do the results demonstrate? Do they back up the idea of interference in LTM?
- Does this experiment demonstrate retroactive or proactive interference?
- Evaluate the findings of this experiment.
- Give some everyday examples of retroactive interference and proactive interference.

Notes

- McGeoch & McDonald (1931) found that Group A participants remembered 4.51 adjectives with the ten minute rest, Group B participants remembered 3.68 with the number interference task and Group C only remembered 1.25 words when asked to learn list 2.

Homework

Look up the following website and participate in the experiments there.
http://olias.arc.nasa.gov/cognition/tutorials/Interference/auindex.html
Make notes from the text which explain how the experiments you participated in demonstrate the role of interference in STM. You will need a PC with sound for this activity.

Essential reading

Gross, McIlveen *et al.* (2000), pages 31–33 and then complete the 'Pause for thought' activity.

Activity 12   Does retrieval-failure theory explain aspects of forgetting?

Objective

To investigate the effect of retrieval cues on memory recall.

Introduction

One of the explanations for forgetting (or remembering) is that the correct memories cannot be accessed because the correct retrieval cues are not being used. This is called the retrieval-failure theory. There are two simple activities that can be conducted which demonstrate the importance of retrieval cues for memory.

Activity 12a **Where is that memory?**

Objective

To investigate the effect that context plays on memory recall.

Introduction

One aspect of cue-dependent forgetting is context-dependent forgetting. Research appears to show that it is easier to recall material if you are in the same context in which you originally learnt it. Godden & Baddeley (1975) conducted a classic study involving divers learning either on land or underwater. Recall was 30 per cent worse for those who had to recall material in a different context.

Materials

Two different contexts (e.g. classroom and field or car park); list of 20 nouns.

HOW DO YOU DO IT?

Devise a word list of 20 common, everyday nouns. Tell your participants that their task is to learn the list. Read out your list to your participants and then randomly divide participants into two groups. One group must then go to a different context (the more different the better) and once there, recall the 20 words. The remaining participants can stay in the original learning context and recall the words there.
Compare the recall scores of the 'same context' group with the 'different context' group.

- There are a number of problems with this procedure. Evaluate the procedure you used and the findings of this experiment. What controls should have been accounted for? Write out an improved design for the study.
- What do the results demonstrate? Do they back up the idea of context-dependent memory?
- Give some everyday examples of context-dependent memory. Could you use this knowledge to help with your exam preparation? In what way(s)?
- Although many textbooks imply that context-dependent findings are robust and reliable there are a number of studies (Fernandez and Glenberg) in which reliable effects have not been found. What does Baddeley (1995) say about this?

Notes

You could try a similar study but this time investigate the effect of state-dependent memory. The term 'state' refers to different psychological or physiological variables (such as emotions or mood) which vary between the learning and recalling state.

Homework

Write up your method and results from the context-dependent study you carried out. You may wish to read the section 'How to write up coursework' prior to this (300 words maximum).

Essential reading

Read Gross, McIlveen *et al.* (2000), pages 30–31 to consolidate your learning.

A*ctivity 12b* Do category cues help memory recall?

Objective

To investigate whether having material organised into categories helps memory coding and subsequent recall.

Introduction

Retrieval cues may help to locate information which is otherwise inaccessible in memory. The activity below is a simple adaptation of an experiment by Tulving & Pearlstone (1966) who demonstrated this effect.

Materials

Word lists shown below.

HOW DO YOU DO IT?

Half of the participants should read list one and the other half should read list two below. They shold be read *twice* at normal reading speed. They should *not* see the other version of the list.

Word list one:

Hut captain rose whisky zinc cliff mountain drill cottage corporal daffodil gin aluminium river saw tent sergeant violet vodka hill chisel hotel colonel orchid rum copper volcano nail boat lieutenant pansy wine iron valley spanner shed private daisy brandy gold hammer

Word list two: *(Hint: Read in column order.)*

hut	cliff	captain	rose	zinc	whisky	drill
cottage	river	corporal	daffodil	aluminium	gin	saw
tent	hill	sergeant	violet	bronze	vodka	chisel
boat	valley	lieutenant	pansy	iron	wine	spanner
shed	mountain	private	daisy	gold	brandy	hammer

The group who read List one should be given a blank sheet of paper to recall all of the words and the other half of your participants should be given a piece of paper which contains the seven categories that the 42 words come from, i.e.

Dwellings   Natural features   Military ranks   Flowers   Metals   Alcoholic drinks   Tools

It is predicted that these category cues should help recall.

- Write out a suitable one-tailed experimental hypothesis for this study.
- Compare the number of words that the two groups recalled.
- Copy Figure 2.9 on page 31 of Gross, McIlveen *et al.* (2000) and add your own results to it.
- Explain these findings in the light of retrieval-failure theory.
- What applications might such findings have for your own revision strategies?
- You could give Group 1 the category headings after their first attempt and see if their recall improves.

Notes

- This study showed that category cues help recall *after* material has been learnt. Categorising material *prior* to learning has also been shown to be an effective memory strategy. You could try this variation if you wish.
- You might like to replicate the 'tip of the tongue' experiment by Brown & McNeil (1966) described in Gross, McIlveen *et al.* (2000), Box 2.10, page 30, which also demonstrates the importance of retrieval cues. You would need a dictionary to do this.

Homework

Using your textbook, outline the follow-up study that Tulving (1968) conducted and explain how this supported the retrieval-failure theory (maximum 100 words).

Website

Read the essay on this topic at http://www.ntu.ac.uk/soc/bscpsych/memory/revise.htm. Print it out or summarise it for your file.

Essential reading

Read Gross, McIlveen *et al.* (2000), pages 30–31.

Activity 13 Recalling 'flashbulb' memories

Objective

To understand the concept of 'flashbulb' memories.

Introduction

Flashbulb memories are specific types of memory which are recalled extremely vividly. Flashbulb memories are referred to in the specification with regard to emotional factors in forgetting.

HOW DO YOU DO IT?

Rubin & Kozin (1984) asked people to recall their three clearest and most vivid memories. The most often recalled memories were personal to them and did not include national events. Emotional factors and the number of times people had recalled these memories seemed implicated in their memorability.

- Write down your three clearest 'flashbulb' memories.
- Are they similar to those reported by Rubin and Kozin? This may be due to 'demand characteristics'. What are demand characteristics?
- Was there an emotional element or heightened level of arousal connected with any of the memories?
- If possible, check with a friend or relative how accurate these memories are.

Notes

Studies of flashbulb memories can also be included as providing critical evidence against Atkinson and Shiffrin's multi-store model. The multi-store model takes little account of the nature or quality of the memory being stored. A flashbulb memory may become embedded in LTM for life despite not being rehearsed within STM. Other information that the STM rehearses over and over again may never become permanently stored in LTM.

Variation

- Students could interview each other about their clearest flashbulb memories. They would have to decide which type of interview was most suitable and what type of questions to ask. They could choose a factual memory, such as the death of Diana where they might be able to check on the accuracy of some of the details that the students recalled.
- Students could try an enhanced cognitive interview technique to see if this helps participants with their memories.

Homework

Using your textbook, summarise what psychologists know about flashbulb memories. Pay particular attention to the study by Wright (1993) who found evidence that people reconstruct events after they have occurred and therefore bring into question the reliability of flashbulb memories (200 words maximum).

Essential reading

Gross, McIlveen *et al.* (2000), pages 34–35.

Activity 14 The effect of leading questions on eyewitness testimony

Notes

You do need to do some preparatory work collecting materials before attempting this task.

Objective

To demonstrate the effect (mis)leading questions can have on eyewitness testimony.

Introduction

There are many studies that have shown that eyewitness memories can be unreliable. A classic study was conducted by Loftus & Zanni (1975) which showed that eyewitnesses' memories can be affected by the type of questions subjects are asked after witnessing the event.

Materials

A three-minute video of a bank robbery or car crash. You could record an incident from 'The Bill' television programme. There is a suitable staged robbery on the Uniview 'Memory' video.

- Ten questions about the video incident.
- Five additional 'leading' questions and five 'open' questions.

HOW DO YOU DO IT?

Once you have found an appropriate video clip, you need to devise ten questions about the incident. For example:

- What was the make of the getaway car?
- What was its licence number?
- How many customers were in the bank?

All participants will have to answer these 'neutral' questions.

Next, you need to devise five further questions which can be made into either leading or open questions. These are the critical questions. For example:

Leading questions	*Open questions*
What was the road sign by the car?	Was there a road sign by the car?
Which robber hit a customer?	Did any robber hit a customer?
How many shots were fired?	Were any shots fired?

Make up two question sheets. One sheet should ask the ten neutral questions with the five leading questions mixed in randomly; the other should ask the neutral and open questions.
Ask the participants to watch the video (e.g. bank robbery).
Half the participants should be given the leading set of questions and half the open set of question to answer. They must not be aware that there are two slightly different versions of the questionnaire.

- Compare the two groups' answers to the critical questions only. What do the results demonstrate?
- Make notes on the Loftus & Palmer (1974) study described in Box 2.15 on page 39 of Gross, McIlveen *et al.* (2000).
- What other factors have been shown to affect eyewitness testimony? (Give at least four.)

Homework

Evaluate Loftus' research. Mention the Yuille & Cutshall (1986) study in your answer (200 words).

Website references

- http://faculty.washington.edu/eloftus/
  A site by Elizabeth Loftus with a picture of her, some EWT articles and a list of books she has authored. Includes her e-mail address if you think you might get a reply!

Essential reading

Read Gross, McIlveen *et al.* (2000), pages 39–40.

Activity 15 'The War of the Ghosts' serial reproduction task

Objective

To understand the processes involved in reconstructive memory using the serial reproduction method.

Introduction

Bartlett (1932) proposed that to study memory it was best to use meaningful material rather than ask participants to learn and recall nonsense syllables (as Ebbinghaus did). Bartlett used a North American folk tale to demonstrate how people 'reconstruct' memories.

Materials

'War of the Ghosts' story, pen and paper.

HOW DO YOU DO IT?

Read the 'War of the Ghosts' passage. A copy is reproduced in Gross, R., *Psychology: The Science of Mind and Behaviour*, 4th edition (2001) Hodder and Stoughton.
Now try to write down the story in as much detail as possible. Pass this new version on to the next participant for them to read and then recall. Repeat the procedure until each participant has read a version of the story and tried to recall it. Each new version is a reproduction of the one they read which is why this technique is called 'serial reproduction'. (The technique resembles the game 'Chinese whispers').

- What were your results and how did they compare to Bartlett's findings?
- Why did he use such an unusual story?
- Have follow-up studies found similar results?
- What can you infer about the schemata that the participants were using, which helps to account for the distortion that took place?
- How can we link Bartlett's research findings to eyewitness testimony memories?

Notes

- Bartlett concluded that interpretation plays a major role in remembering. 'Active' processes employ *'effort after meaning'* which involves trying to make the past more logical, coherent and sensible. We reconstruct the past by trying to fit it into our existing understanding of the world. Bartlett called this existing understanding of the world a 'schema'.
- The plural for 'schema' is either 'schemas' or 'schemata'!

Homework

Describe and evaluate the schema theory of memory (100 words maximum).

Essential reading:

Read Gross, McIlveen *et al.* (2000), pages 36–37 to consolidate your learning.

Activity 16 How schemata affect our thinking

Objective

To demonstrate how pre-existing schemata play a large part in our interpretation of material such as stories and events.

Introduction

Bartlett concluded that schemata provide us with ready made expectations, make the world more predictable, help with 'filling in the gaps' of information and can therefore produce significant distortions in the memory process.

Materials

Lateral puzzles below.

HOW DO YOU DO IT?

Three lateral thinking puzzles are outlined below. Read out each one and ask participants to write down their answers/responses. They could shout out their answers but, if correct, it spoils it for the rest of the group.

Puzzle 1
A man stood looking through the window on the ninth floor of an office building. Suddenly, he was overcome by an impulse. He opened the window and leapt through it. It was a sheer drop outside the building to the pavement below. He did not have a parachute or land on any special soft surface yet he was completely unhurt when he landed. Explain what happened.

Puzzle 2
A man walked home after having been out drinking. He walked down the middle of a deserted country road. There were no street lights to illuminate the road and there was no moonlight. He was dressed completely in black. Suddenly, a car that did not have its headlights on came racing down the road. At the last moment, the driver saw the man and swerved to avoid him. How did he manage to see him?

Puzzle 3
Geoff and Billy were professional golfers and keen rivals. One day, during a game, when they had both scored 30, Geoff hit a particularly bad shot and Billy added 10 to his own score. Billy then hit a good shot and declared that he had won the game. Why?

- Ask for volunteers to read out their answers. Participants' inability to explain are likely due to pre-existing schemata.
- Reread the original puzzles and see if they have added in or missed important information.
- Ask if any of the participants know of puzzles along similar lines.

Notes

This is a light hearted activity but it can be used to lead into a discussion about schema theory, reconstructive memory and the accuracy of eyewitness testimony.

Answers

Puzzle 1: He was originally on the outside on the window ledge contemplating suicide and jumped into the building.
Puzzle 2: People wrongly assume the man was coming home at night. In fact, he was returning home in broad daylight.
Puzzle 3: They were playing tennis, not golf as many people assume.

Activity 17 **Memory spidergram**

Objective

To enhance student knowledge of memory and see how the topics involving memory interact.

Introduction

Memory is obviously a very complicated phenomenon and usually referred to by 'lay' people as one overall concept or process. However, for the purposes of study it helps to break such a huge topic down into smaller units. The danger with this approach is that it is more difficult to see how each area connects to the others. A summary spidergram can often help.

HOW DO YOU DO IT?

Work in pairs and write the word 'memory' in the middle of an A3 sheet of paper. Look at the topics below and position them on your paper, showing the links (if any) between them.

Short term memory	Long term memory
Multi-store model of memory	Working memory model
Levels of processing model	Forgetting in STM
Decay	Displacement
Forgetting in LTM	Retrieval failure
Interference	Emotional factors
Flashbulb memories	Repression
Reconstructive memory	Bartlett's 'War of the Ghosts'
Freud	Elizabeth Loftus
Face recognition	

If possible include a key name or research study for each topic listed above.
Show your spidergram to the rest of the class and explain the links you have made.

Notes

There is no correct scheme for the links between the topics. With a topic such as memory it may be possible to make links between many of the topics, it is the explanations for the links that are important to demonstrate student understanding of the whole area of memory.

Activity 18 Revision summary: Memory

Define memory.

What is encoding?

What is the capacity of STM?

What is the duration of STM?

What is the capacity of LTM?

What is the duration of LTM?

Who produced the multi-store model?

Who produced the working memory model?

Who produced the levels of processing model?

Explain what is meant by memory decay.

Explain what is meant by memory displacement.

Explain what is meant by memory retrieval failure.

Explain what is meant by memory interference (include the terms retroactive and proactive interference).

Explain what is meant by the term flashbulb memory.

Explain what is meant by the term repression.

What does the term reconstructive memory refer to?

What is meant by face recognition?

Activity 19 Memory revision exercise

Putting each item on a single, separate side of A4 ...
describe the aims/procedures/findings/conclusions/two criticisms of ONE study:

- into the capacity of STM
- which shows a difference between STM and LTM
- of flashbulb memories
- which supports the multi-store model
- which supports the working memory model
- which supports the levels of processing model
- which explains the theory of decay
- which supports the theory of displacement
- which has explored the role of repression
- that has explored the nature of reconstructive memory
- carried out by Loftus in the area of eyewitness testimony
- into face recognition.

Activity 20 Multiple choice test

1 Who started the scientific study of memory in 1885?
   a Ebbinghaus
   b Bartlett
   c Eysenck
   d Flanagan

2 Encoding:
   a involves the transformation of a sensory input into a form which allows it to be entered into memory
   b is the process by which stored information is extracted from memory
   c is the holding of information in memory
   d is the inability to recall information from memory.

3 Retrieval:
   a involves the transformation of a sensory input into a form which allows it to be entered into memory
   b is the process by which stored information is extracted from memory
   c is the holding of information in memory
   d is the inability to recall information from memory.

4 Storage:
   a involves the transformation of a sensory input into a form which allows it to be entered into memory
   b is the process by which stored information is extracted from memory
   c is the holding of information in memory
   d is the inability to recall information from memory.

5 Availability refers to:
   a whether or not information is stored in the first place
   b whether there is sufficient brain space available to register the memory
   c whether or not information can be retrieved
   d whether one knows the information that must be registered.

6 Accessibility refers to:
   a whether or not information is stored in the first place
   b whether there is sufficient brain space available to register the memory
   c whether or not information can be retrieved
   d whether one knows the information that must be registered.

7 The capacity of STM is:
   a 5 ± 2
   b 6 ± 2
   c 7 ± 2
   d 8 ± 2.

8 STM coding is predominantly:
   a visual
   b acoustic
   c semantic
   d echoic.

9 LTM coding is predominantly:
a visual
b acoustic
c semantic
d echoic.

10 The multi-store model was proposed by:
a Atkinson and Shiffrin
b Eysenck
c Baddeley
d Craik and Lockhart.

11 Shallice & Warington supported the multi-store model with their case study of:
a GW
b HM
c HP
d KF.

12 The working memory model was proposed by:
a Atkinson and Shiffrin
b Eysenck
c Baddeley and Hitch
d Craik and Lockhart.

13 Components of the working memory model include the visual spatial scratch pad, the articulatory or phonological loop and the:
a central executive
b semantic store
c elaborative store
d semantic scratch pad.

14 Who proposed the levels of processing model?
a Atkinson and Shiffrin
b Eysenck
c Baddeley
d Craik and Lockhart

15 In Jenkins and Dallenbach's experiment recall was:
a better after sleeping
b worse after sleeping
c better after staying awake
d better after a psychology lesson.

16 The Jenkins and Dallenbach study supported:
a trace decay
b interference
c displacement
d retrieval-failure theory.

17 'Flashbulb' memory refers to a special kind of:
a semantic memory
b episodic memory
c phonemic memory
d acoustic memory.

18 Repression refers to:
   a depressed people's memory recall
   b forgetting which occurs in the absence of relevant environmental or contextual variables
   c an unconscious process in which some memories are made inaccessible
   d failure to learn material adequately.

19 Retroactive interference is where:
   a learning is affected by the passage of time
   b the learning of a first list interferes with recall of a second
   c learning of old material is pushed out by new material
   d the learning of a second list interferes with recall of the first.

20 In Loftus & Palmer's (1974) study on the effect of leading questions on judgement of car speed, which word produced the highest speed estimate?
   a contacted
   b smashed
   c hit
   d bumped

Answers to Activity 20

1 a
2 a
3 b
4 c
5 a
6 c
7 c
8 b
9 c
10 a
11 d
12 c
13 a
14 d
15 a
16 b
17 b
18 c
19 d
20 b

2 Developmental Psychology: Attachments in Development

Specification topic	Gross, McIlveen et al. (2000) 2nd edition	Activity	Page
The development and variety of attachments	44–65		
• Development of attachments (Schaffer)	45	21 Sociability	37
• Research into individual differences Secure and insecure attachments (Ainsworth)	49–52	22 Individual differences in attachment	38
• Explanations of attachment Bowlby's theory	45–49	23 Support for Bowlby's theory	41
Deprivation and privation	53–61		
• Research into the *short* term effects of deprivation / separation. • Bowlby's maternal deprivation hypothesis.	53–55	24 Effects of short-term separation	42
• Research into long term effects of deprivation / separation	56–57	25 Effects of privation 26 Effects of long-term separation (divorce)	45 47
• Privation	57–58	27 Privation	49
• Hodges and Tizard's study of institutionalisation.	58–59	28 Institutionalisation	51
Day care	61–64		
• Types of day care.	61		
• Effects of day care on social development.	63	29 Social development	53
Revision summary	44–65	30 Overview of early socialisation	54
• Multiple choice questions		31 Multiple choice questions	55

General textbooks

1 **Gross, R., McIlveen, R. *et al.*** (2000) 2nd edition, *Psychology: A New Introduction*. Hodder & Stoughton.
2 **Gross, R. & McIlveen, R.** (1998) 1st edition, *Psychology: A New Introduction*. Hodder & Stoughton.
3 **Gross, R.** (1996) 3rd edition, *Psychology: The Science of Mind and Behaviour*. Hodder & Stoughton.
4 **Gross, R.** (1995) 2nd edition, *Themes, Issues and Debates in Psychology*, Chapter 9. Hodder & Stoughton.

Activity 21 Sociability

Objective

To show that sociability is an integral part of attachment.

Introduction

Sociability is the predisposition of an infant to seek social interaction. Attachment is the enduring emotional relationship between the infant and mother or another caregiver. This activity covers the ways the infant reacts to and interacts with the mother. This interaction involves the effect the one has on the other. It implies that some form of communication is taking place. It is a two way process. What form does this communication take and how early does it start?

HOW DO YOU DO IT?

In groups of two:

- Imagine for a moment that you are a very young baby, with no language or motor control.
  How would you express yourself?
  How might you have some control over the people in your environment?
  Write down your ideas.
- With a fellow student, attempt to express yourself using only facial expressions.
  Show happiness, sadness, joy, anger, frustration, discomfort and any others you think possible.
  Your fellow student has to write down the expressions that they think you are communicating.
- Swap roles and see if your partner can do any better.
- Which expressions, made by a baby, do you think could be identified by the mother, father or caregiver?

Notes

- A further activity could involve using a camcorder to film a baby's expressions and show it in class for general discussion and analysis. Parental permission must be obtained and all ethical guidelines must be followed.
- See Gross *Psychology* (1996) 3rd edition, pages 120–121 for a relevant study by Ekman & Friesen (1975).

Homework

- If it is possible, spend time with a very young baby and try to identify the child's expressions. Record the stimulus you used in each case and the baby's response.
- Ask the mother, father or caregiver what they think the child is expressing. Record their view.
- To whom was the baby most responsive? Explain your answer.
- Which adult was most sensitive to the baby? Explain your answer.

Essential reading

Gross, McIlveen *et al.* (2000), page 45.

Activity 22 Individual differences in attachment

Objective

To investigate individual differences in child rearing styles and their effect on attachment.

Introduction

Mary Ainsworth worked with John Bowlby on the nature of attachments. Both recognised that there was a difference between infants in the nature of their attachments. The majority of children formed secure attachments and went on to be balanced and happy adults. However, a minority became either anxious or resistant in their relationship with their mother or primary caregiver, and this may have had a long-term effect.

HOW DO YOU DO IT?

Work in groups of two, three or four.

Think about the range of issues over which parents disagree on how to bring up children. Some examples are given below. Now try to fill in the possible effect on attachment for each example on the response sheet.

Child rearing issues		*Possible effect on attachment*
Sleeping arrangements?	Own bedroom	(e.g. increases independence)
	With mother/parents	
Rules for bedtimes?	Rigid and regular	
	Relaxed and inconsistent	
Breastfeeding?	Prolonged breastfeeding	
	Early on the bottle	
Diet?	Organic food	
	Junk food	
Mealtime discipline?	No nonsense	
	Fun time	
Toilet training?	Negative reinforcement	
	Punishment	
	Positive reinforcement	
Smacking?	Indiscriminately	(e.g. leads to anxiety)
	Never	

Can you think of any other issues in addition to the list above?

Try to answer these questions:

- Are there expectations about how soon a toddler should start walking?
- Are some parents too pushy?
- Does this matter?
- Does the same apply to how soon a child should start talking?
- Are some parents over anxious about the development of their child? Does this matter?
- Do other parents hold back from stimulating their child in learning to speak? What effect might this have?

Notes

Van Ijzendoorn & Kroonenberg (1988) used Ainsworth's 'strange situation' study and applied it to several countries around the world. See Gross, McIlveen *et al.* (2000), page 43.

Homework

Ask your mum, dad or step-parent, and a grandparent what was the fashionable way to bring up children when they did so. Use the range of issues chosen in the activity. (Word limit 150.)

Essential reading

Gross, McIlveen *et al.* (2000), pages 49–51.

Website reference

http://www.psychology.sunysb.edu/ewaters
This will provide a wealth of information on attachment theory and research.

Activity 22 **Response sheet**

Child rearing issues		Possible effect on attachment
Sleeping arrangements?	Own bedroom With mother/parents	(e.g. increases independence).
Rules for bedtimes?	Rigid and regular Relaxed and inconsistent	
Breastfeeding?	Prolonged breastfeeding Early on the bottle	
Diet?	Organic food Junk food	
Mealtime discipline?	No nonsense Fun time	
Toilet training?	Negative reinforcement Punishment Positive reinforcement	
Smacking?	Indiscriminately Never	(e.g. leads to anxiety)

Can you think of any other issues in addition to the list above?

1

2

Try to answer these questions:

- Are there expectations about how soon a toddler should start walking?
- Are some parents too pushy?
- Does this matter?
- Does the same apply to how soon a child should start talking?
- Are some parents over anxious about the development of their child? Does this matter?
- Do other parents hold back from stimulating their child in learning to speak?
- What effect might this have?

Activity 23 Support for Bowlby's theory of attachment

Objective

To study evidence of examples in the non-human animal world in support of Bowlby's theory of attachment.

Introduction

Bowlby argued that newborn infants are genetically programmed to behave in ways to maximise their survival. Mothers too are programmed to respond to their baby. There will be a pattern of behaviour involving how much distance each will move away from the other. Human babies will explore their world away from the secure base of their mother. A mother will leave her baby in a safe place to go off to do essential jobs. It has been discovered that female giraffes leave their offspring in the shade during the day.

HOW DO YOU DO IT?

Working individually, find the website http://www.johnbowlby.com
Go to 'Images & Artefacts' and 'Gallery' and 'Shady Deal'.
Read the article on the screen or print the three pages for your file.
Answer the following questions from the article:

1 What are the two imperatives that challenge the giraffes?
2 How often do the mothers feed their infants each day?
3 Does a mother leave the infant completely unprotected?
4 Why does an infant giraffe have to stay in the shade?
5 Why do several infant giraffes group together?
6 Why don't the mothers stay with their offspring?
7 In what ways might human mothers show similar behaviour?
8 Is it a mistake to generalise from giraffes to humans?

Notes

The work of Lorenz (1935) influenced Bowlby and this can be researched in reading and homework.

Homework

Explain how Lorenz's work with goslings influenced Bowlby's theory of attachment (word limit 300).

Essential reading

• Read Bowlby's theory on page 48 of Gross, McIlveen *et al.* (2000).
• Read Lorenz's research on page 47 of Gross, McIlveen *et al.* (2000).

Website reference

http://www.johnbowlby.com
This site contains a very wide range of material on attachment, especially Mary Ainsworth's research.

Activity 24 Effects of short-term separation

Objective:

To explore the causes and consequences of short-term separation.

Introduction:

The stimulus material comes from James and Joyce Robertson (1969). The details of the stages of protest, despair and detachment can be seen in Box 3.8, page 47 in Gross, McIlveen *et al.* (2000). This activity is a close parallel to those comments.

HOW DO YOU DO IT?

Working in small groups, try to describe from your own feelings or observations of others, what it is like for a young child to be separated for a few days from a special person, especially a mother or caregiver.

If it helps, think of events in your own life or those of a younger brother or sister, or a toddler in your circle of family or friends. (Use the table on the next page to answer the questions below.) Three stages of separation behaviour have been identified:

Protest	Despair	Detachment
Describe how a child would show their feelings on separation.	How would the lonely child show a negative attitude?	If the separation continues the child responds to people differently by treating everyone alike and rather superficially.
Tears?	Facial expression?	Facial expression?
Voice?	Voice?	Voice?
Gestures?	Gestures?	Gestures?
Tantrums?	Body posture?	Behaviour?
What do these behaviours suggest about what is going on inside the child?	What do these behaviours suggest about what is going on inside the child?	When reunited with the mother the child *might* react with little joy.
Upset or anger?	Bottling up sadness or in control?	Disinterested or delighted?
Concern or fear?	Helplessness or braving it out?	Turning away or towards her?
Grumpy or bitter?	Sulky or just independent?	Rejecting her or hugging her?

Think how individual differences may account for the different ways in which children react to separation, for example:

- with securely attached children
- with anxious avoidant children
- with anxious resistant children.

Look back at the three types of attachment described by Mary Ainsworth in the 'strange situation experiment'.

Notes

The effects of long-term deprivation can be seen in Box 3.9, page 48 of Gross, McIlveen *et al.* (2000).

Homework

See Figure 3.9 on page 47 of Gross, McIlveen *et al.* (2000). How could John be helped to cope with the separation of his mother for the days she was away in hospital? (Word limit 50.)

Essential reading

- Box 3.8, page 47 in Gross, McIlveen *et al.* (2000).
- Table 3.2, page 51 in Gross, McIlveen *et al.* (2000).

Activity 24 **Response sheet**

Effects of short-term separation

Protest	Despair	Detachment
Describe how a child would show their feelings on separation.	How would the lonely child show a negative attitude?	If the separation continues the child responds to people differently by treating everyone alike and rather superficially.
Tears?	Facial expression?	Facial expression?
Voice?	Voice?	Voice?
Gestures?	Gestures?	Gestures?
Tantrums?	Body posture?	Behaviour?
What do these behaviours suggest about what is going on inside the child?	What do these behaviours suggest about what is going on inside the child?	When reunited with the mother the child might react with little joy.
Upset or anger?	Bottling up sadness or in control?	Disinterested or delighted?
Concern or fear?	Helplessness or braving it out?	Turning away or towards her?
Grumpy or bitter?	Sulky or just independent?	Rejecting her or hugging her?
Think how individual differences may account for the different ways in which children react to separation.		
Securely attached children:	anxious avoidant children:	anxious resistant children:

Activity 25 Effects of privation

Objective

To assess the different research evidence for the effects of privation.

Introduction

Privation is the absence of any primary caregiver in the first place. Both privation and long-term separation (as in family break-up) may result in children receiving full-time care in residential nurseries and orphanages. Bowlby's maternal deprivation hypothesis was based on early studies of children in institutional care. Other later studies offered different interpretations of long-term deprivation and challenged his conclusions on this research.

HOW DO YOU DO IT?

Bowlby proposed his maternal deprivation hypothesis in the light of his own research and that of others. However, his hypothesis is not supported by later research conducted in the 1970s. Working in small groups, use the table on the next page to show the evidence for either side of the debate.

Evidence for the maternal deprivation hypothesis		Evidence against the maternal deprivation hypothesis	
Research name/s	Research details	Research name/s	Research details
1 Goldfarb (1943)	1	1 Schaffer & Emerson (1964)	1
2 Spitz & Wolf (1945)	2	2 Rutter (1981)	2
3 Bowlby (1946)	3	3 Suomi & Harlow (1977)	3

Make some evaluation about these studies. Write concisely (one sentence) on each point. Consider the following factors in your evaluation:

1 Are some of these retrospective studies too out-of-date?
2 Mention a disadvantage with the use of small samples.
3 Is there a problem with biased samples anywhere?
4 Are there any reasons, other than maternal deprivation, for the later behavioural problems?
5 How accurate is the information from the families involved in such studies?
6 Do any of these studies confuse deprivation with privation?
7 What cross-cultural issues are involved in any other of these studies?

Notes

Activity 26 takes the effects of long-term deprivation and privation in the context of the issues of parental death and divorce.

Homework

Critically consider Bowlby's maternal deprivation hypothesis (word limit 150).

Essential reading

Gross, McIlveen *et al.* (2000), pages 45–58.

Activity 25 **Response sheet**

Evidence for the maternal deprivation hypothesis		Evidence against the maternal deprivation hypothesis	
Research name/s	Research details	Research name/s	Research details
1 Goldfarb (1943)		**1** Schaffer & Emerson (1964)	
2 Spitz & Wolf (1945)		**2** Rutter (1981)	
3 Bowlby (1946)		**3** Suomi & Harlow (1977)	

Activity 26 Effects of long-term separation (divorce)

Objective

To assess the effects of parental death and divorce.

Introduction

Long-term deprivation includes the permanent separation resulting from parental *death* and the increasingly common separation caused by *divorce*. The fear that separation will occur again in the future was called *separation anxiety* by Bowlby. Conflict is likely to be present before divorce and can even increase after divorce. However, there may be greater harmony in a new household after divorce.

HOW DO YOU DO IT?

Read the following article.

Divorce hits families harder than death

The damage to children caused by marital conflict occurs long before divorce and persists long after it, according to British and American surveys.

The studies show that years before parents separate there are clear differences in their children: they perform less well at school and have more behavioural problems than the children of unbroken families.

Dr Kathleen Kiernan, of the Department of Population Studies at the London School of Economics, said, 'Divorce is a process that starts long before the separation itself occurs. It is what goes on in families that is important.'

Speaking yesterday in London at a conference on young people and divorce, organised by the Trust for the Study of Adolescence, Dr Kiernan said that the effects, on children, of marital breakdown extended far into adulthood. 'Evidence is beginning to accrue which suggests that children from lone-parent families and particularly step-families are more likely to leave home at a young age and for negative reasons, such as conflict and friction.'

Children of divorced parents did less well at school, had lower incomes and less prestigious occupations. But, Dr Kiernan said, it was impossible to say whether it was the divorce or the marital conflict that led to the children's difficulties, because there were no data available on families who continued to live in conflict but did not break up. The poverty associated with divorce could not explain all the differences.

Dr Kiernan, who has analysed findings from the National Child Development Study of 11,000 children born in 1958 and now aged 35, said that children who lost a parent through death did not under-perform in the same way as children who lost a parent through divorce. 'It is easier to maintain a family and social support network after a death than it is after a divorce,' she said.

Jan Walker, director of the Family and Community Dispute Research Centre in Newcastle upon Tyne, said that most fathers struggled hard to maintain their relationship with their children after divorce but were sometimes defeated by overwhelming odds. In a study of 91 fathers, the centre found that three quarters had maintained contact with their children and were paying maintenance five years after divorce.

'We did not find a single father who had given up on his children because he didn't care,' Ms Walker said, 'Some did give up, but only after a tremendous struggle. Divorce is not a happy time and if there is ongoing bitterness and conflict it is hard to maintain contact.'

Author: Jeremy Laurance
Source: *The Times*, 9 October 1993

Answer these questions based on the article above:

1 Over what period of time can divorce damage some children?
2 How are the negative effects of marital conflict measured?
3 What is another effect on children 'from lone-parent families and particularly step-families'?
4 Name three consequences of divorced parents.
5 Why is it impossible to say whether it was the divorce or marital conflict that led to the children's difficulties?
6 According to Kiernan's findings, what is the difference between children who lost a parent through death and children who lost a parent through divorce?
7 What was the more positive picture about divorced fathers in Walker's study?
8 Is there a possible positive scenario about divorce, which is left out of this article?

Notes

Similar articles from research quoted in newspapers could be found and are available on CD-ROMs.

Homework

How many of the issues raised in this article are as true today as they were in 1993? (Word limit 150.)

Essential reading

Gross, McIlveen *et al.* (2000), pages 56–57.

Website

http://www.bereavement.org.uk
This is the London Bereavement Network site, with details of contacts and support.

Activity 27 Privation

Objective

To compare and contrast three studies of privation.

Introduction

Privation is the lack or absence of an attachment figure. This is different from deprivation, which is the loss of, or separation from, an attachment figure. Deprivation has short-term effects such as distress and long-term effects such as separation anxiety. It is assumed that attachment has already taken place in cases of deprivation, but in privation no attachment has formed in the first place. Privation has more serious long-term effects of developmental retardation, such as affectionless psychopathy.

HOW DO YOU DO IT?

- See Figure 3.7 on page 54 Gross, McIlveen *et al.* (2000).
  Read the comments underneath the picture, which refer to studies similar to those in Romanian orphanages (Chisolm *et al.* 1995).
- See Box 3.11 on page 57 of Gross, McIlveen *et al.* (2000).
  Read the study of 44 juvenile thieves (Bowlby 1946).
- See Box 3.12 on page 58 of Gross, McIlveen *et al.* (2000).
  Read the case of PM and JM, identical twin boys from Czechoslovakia (Koluchova 1972).
- In groups of two, three or four discuss the five issues listed below.
- Use the table on the next page to write down your answers.

	English juveniles	Czechoslovakian twins	Romanian orphans
1 Summary of study			
2 Quality of environment			
3 Quality of attachment			
4 Sample size			
5 Other factors			

Notes

Contrasts and comparisons can be made from a range of additional research examples on privation to be found in psychological literature.

Homework

Is it possible to make general conclusions based on these three studies? (Word limit 50.)

Essential reading

- See Figure 3.7 on page 54 of Gross, McIlveen *et al.* (2000).
- See Box 3.11 on page 57 of Gross, McIlveen *et al.* (2000).
- See Box 3.12 on page 58 of Gross, McIlveen *et al.* (2000).

Activity 27 Response sheet

English juveniles	Czechoslovakian twins	Romanian orphans
1 Summary of study	1 Summary of study	1 Summary of study
2 Quality of environment	2 Quality of environment	2 Quality of environment
3 Quality of attachment	3 Quality of attachment	3 Quality of attachment
4 Sample size	4 Sample size	4 Sample size
5 Other factors a b	5 Other factors a b	5 Other factors a b

Activity 28 Institutionalisation

Objective

To study the effects of institutionalisation and other options.

Introduction

Children may be raised in either their natural family, adopted family or in institutional care; whichever, it is hoped that the quality of care is consistently high. However, if there is lack of good quality care in any circumstance, there could be adverse effects in the short term and the long term. Hodges & Tizard (1989) studied working class children who had been cared for in a residential nursery in their first two years. In a longitudinal study the children were assessed at 4½-, 8- and 16-years-old and compared with a control group of children from a similar background who had been cared for at home. Most of the children from institutional care had been adopted or returned to their biological families at between 2- and 7-years-old. Further comparisons were made between these different patterns of social and family relationships.

HOW DO YOU DO IT?

On your own, read the study by Hodges and Tizard on pages 58–59 in Gross, McIlveen *et al.* (2000).
Now read the further details below.

Positive features of the institutional care
The nursery had well-trained staff and high quality care.
The children received good attention.
There were stimulating toys, books and resources.
The children were well fed.

Negative features of the institutional care
High turnover of staff.
Little opportunity for the children to make attachments.
Attachments between staff and children were discouraged.

Positive results of the institutional care (at 16 years)
Adopted children were just as attached to their adopted parents as the control group.
Adopted children were more affectionate with their adopted parents than the returned children.

Negative results of the institutional care (at 16 years)
Returned children were less attached to their natural parents as the control group and the adopted children.
Institutional children, especially the returned children, had more problems with siblings than the control group.
Returned children were less affectionate with their natural parents than the control group.

In pairs, discuss the following questions and write your answers in your own words

1 What were the key issues involving the staff in the institutions?
2 Why did the adopted children show more positive results than the other groups?
3 Why did the returned children fare less well in their own families than the other groups in their families?

Notes

Earlier studies by Bowlby (1951) and Goldfarb (1943) had found that there were short-term and long-term effects with early institutionalisation of children. They gave maternal deprivation as the cause and claimed the effects were irreversible. However, Hodges and Tizard challenged some of these earlier claims and supported their findings with evidence from ex-institution children at 16-years-old.

Homework

Summarise the different views of Bowlby and Hodges and Tizard about the effects of institutionalisation (word limit 150).

Essential reading

Gross, McIlveen *et al.* (2000), pages 58–59.

Website

http://blue.census.gov/population/www/socdemo/childcare.html
An American website from the U.S. Census Bureau giving details of child care arrangements.

Activity 29 Social development

Objective

To consider the effect of care on social development.

Introduction

If day care is well organised, with stimulating and clear, structured tasks, this should contribute positively to the child's social development. Such care should encourage children to get along with others and learn how to gain social skills. This would include their emotional and moral development.

HOW DO YOU DO IT?

Working in small groups, imagine you were in charge of a group of children in day care. They are in need of some constructive activity. You have been told that role play is a good way of developing a child's relationship with other people.
Write your answers down to the following ideas:

- What evidence is there that role play is beneficial? Mention one or two reasons.
- What themes would you choose for role play or guided play? Discuss possibilities and choose one.
  Example 1: 'being ourselves' which could involve the way children would go about doing their own choice of activity in a particular context. This would encourage children to 'do their own thing', and act independently of others.
  Example 2: 'seeing change' which would apply to the changes that children could see in the people around them during an activity in a particular context. This would encourage children to observe change of behaviour in other people and adapt to it if necessary.
- What context would you choose? (e.g. doctor's surgery, the kitchen.)
  Make a choice and then consider these further questions:

- What equipment would be appropriate and what inappropriate?
- What would the health and safety issues be?
- Why should gender stereotyping be avoided? (e.g. girls and cooking, boys and D.I.Y.)
- Why should political correctness be applied? (e.g. cowboys and indians.)
- Would there be any ethical considerations? (e.g. why would 'cops and robbers' be unacceptable?)

Notes

- Related research is by Clarke, Stewart *et al.* (1994); see Gross, McIlveen *et al.* (2000), page 63.
- Defining the quality of care – Bredekamp (1989); see Gross, McIlveen *et al.* (2000), page 62.

Homework

Give reasons why social development in children is important (word limit 150).

Essential reading

Read Gross, McIlveen *et al.* (2000), page 63, for a general comment on this area of social development.

A *ctivity 30* Overview of early socialisation

Objective

To see the inter-relationships between the different aspects of early socialisation.

Introduction

Students should know what a spider diagram looks like. They should be able to find the interconnections between at least two issues and probably many more. This form of 'mind mapping' should act as revision exercise and perhaps help make sense of attachment as a whole topic.

Materials

A3 paper.

HOW DO YOU DO IT?

Working in small groups, think about how to draw the relationships between different issues of early socialisation.

Write 'Early socialisation' in the middle of your spider diagram. Look at the topics below and put them on your spider diagram showing the links between them. There is no 'correct' order in which to deal with these issues.

Early emotional development	Interactions between infant and caregiver
Early social development	Cross-cultural variations
Attachment	Institutionalisation
Deprivation effects	Cognitive development
Privation effects	Social development
Enrichment effects	Emotional development

- Give explanations for the links that you have made.
- What unexpected relationships did you create?
- Are some issues more important than others?

Notes

There will be positive, negative and perhaps neutral interconnections. These could be drawn as straight, wavy and dotted lines respectively, or using different colours.

Homework

Prepare for a multiple choice test on the whole topic of early socialisation.

Essential reading

Read Gross, McIlveen *et al.* (2000), pages 44–68.

Activity 31 Multiple choice questions

1 Attachment:
   a is being protected by a responsible adult
   b is an enduring emotional relationship between two people
   c when broken for a prolonged time leads to stress and sorrow
   d both b and c.

2 According to Schaffer's phases in the development of attachment, babies:
   a give a social smile to almost anyone at about seven months
   b smile at familiar rather than unfamiliar faces at about seven months
   c develop specific attachments at about seven months
   d all of the above.

3 Ainsworth's (1978) 'strange situation' study showed that babies are:
   a type A (15 per cent), showing indifference to their mothers
   b type B (70 per cent), securely attached to their mothers
   c type C (15 per cent), showing independence from their mothers
   d both a and b.

4 Van Ijzendoorn & Krooenberg's (1988) cross-cultural studies, using the 'strange situation', showed:
   a marked differences within some cultures, such as Japan
   b the overall worldwide pattern was similar to Ainsworth's findings
   c type A is relatively more common in Western European countries
   d all of the above.

5 Bowlby's theory stated that:
   a a baby is genetically programmed to respond to its mother
   b a mother has no genetic predisposition to respond to her baby
   c there is no difference between the mother-figure and another caregiver
   d both a and b.

6 According to the behaviourist theory of attachment:
   a food is a primary reinforcer to the infant
   b a caregiver is a secondary reinforcer to the infant
   c the caregiver acts as a model of behaviour for the infant
   d both a and b.

7 The psychoanalytic theory of attachment:
   a stresses the importance of feeding, especially breastfeeding
   b recognises the oral pleasure a baby receives from breastfeeding
   c is concerned with the caregiver's ability to satisfy instinctual needs
   d all of the above.

8 Harlow's studies with rhesus monkeys and surrogate mothers:
   a supported the 'cupboard love' theories of attachment
   b challenged the 'cupboard love' theories of attachment
   c showed that infants do not have an unlearned need for contact comfort
   d both b and c.

9 Schaffer and Emerson:
   a agreed with Bowlby's monotropy theory
   b demonstrated that multiple attachments were possible
   c said that responsiveness to the infant by the caregiver was unimportant
   d all of the above.

10 Deprivation:
   a is living in an inner city environment
   b does not cause separation anxiety in the long term
   c is the loss or separation of an attachment, causing distress
   d both a and b.

11 Bowlby's maternal-deprivation hypothesis stated that if the maternal attachment was broken in the first few years of life there would be:
   a serious and permanent damage to social development
   b serious and permanent damage to emotional development
   c serious and permanent damage to intellectual development
   d all of the above.

12 Bowlby's work was based on:
   a Goldfarb's study of fostering institutionalised children
   b Rutter's work with children from the Isle of Wight
   c Spitz and Wolf's study of Romanian orphanages
   d both a and c.

13 The effect of short-term deprivation is shown in distress, which involves:
   a protest
   b despair
   c detachment
   d all three of the above.

14 Long-term deprivation occurs when:
   a the child is ill
   b there is a divorce or parental death
   c the mother goes into hospital to have a baby
   d both b and c.

15 Koluchova's study of identical twin boys from Czechoslovakia:
   a showed that the negative effects of privation could be overcome
   b supported Bowlby's work on 44 juvenile delinquents
   c showed the impossibility of recovering from genuine privation
   d none of the above.

16 Hodges and Tizard's study of children who had left institutional care between the ages of two and seven showed that they:
   a had no difficulty forming relationships while in care
   b had formed no close attachments to their adoptive parents
   c had formed close attachments to their adoptive parents
   d both a and c.

17 According to Scarr, day care includes:
   a all non-maternal care of children who reside with parent(s)
   b crèches, day nurseries and childminders
   c nannies and non-resident grandparents
   d all of the above.

18 Questions about day care over recent years have included:
   a how much damage is being done to infants of working mothers?
   b what is the quality and variety of care settings?
   c how do children differ in their responses to day care?
   d all of the above.

19 When defining the quality of day care, the agreed criteria should include:
   a warm, supportive interactions with peers
   b a safe, healthy and stimulating environment
   c a high staff turnover (a measure of the quantity of care support)
   d both a and c.

20 Clarke-Stewart found that with children between two and four years old:
   a day care centres had improved cognitive (and social) development
   b home care with mothers had done better than day care
   c home care with childminders had done better than day care
   d all of the above.

Answers to Activity 31

1 d
2 c
3 d
4 d
5 a
6 d
7 d
8 b
9 b
10 c
11 d
12 a
13 d
14 b
15 a
16 c
17 d
18 d
19 b
20 a

3 *Physiological Psychology: Stress*

Specification topic	Gross, McIlveen et al. (2000) 2nd edition	Activity	Page
Stress as a bodily response	68–73	32 An introduction to the topic of stress	59
• The general adaptation syndrome (Selye)	68–73	33 The physiological response to stress 34 The GAS, Selye (1936)	61 63
• The relationship between stress and physical illness, including cardiovascular disorders and the effects of stress on the immune system	74–78	35 Stress and the immune system	66
Sources of stress	78–84	36 A stress diary	68
• Sources of stress including life changes (e.g. Holmes and Rahe) workplace stresses (work overload and ambiguity)	78–82	37 A case study of workplace stress 38 Stressful life events	70 71
• Individual differences to stress including personality (Friedman and Rosenman), culture and gender	82–84	39 Gender differences in coping with stress	72
Stress management	85–92		
• Physical methods of managing stress (drugs and biofeedback); the strengths and weaknesses of these methods	85–86	40 Managing stress 41 Biofeedback 42 Physical methods of stress management	73 75 76
• Psychological methods of managing stress (Meichenbaum's stress inoculation and Kobasa on increasing hardiness); the strengths and weaknesses of these methods	86–88	43 The ten-minute meditation	78
• Role of 'control' in the perception of stress	88–90	44 Coping with stress 45 The perception of stressful events	80 82
• Additional work		46 Revision summary: Stress 47 Multiple choice questions	83 84

General Textbooks

1 **Gross, R. and McIlveen, R.** (1998) *Psychology: A New Introduction*. Hodder & Stoughton.
2 **Gross, R.** (2001) *Psychology: The Science of Mind and Behaviour*. 4th edition. Hodder & Stoughton.

Activity 32 An introduction to the topic of stress

Objective

To discuss sources of stress, effects of stress, managing stress and ways of measuring stress.

Introduction

This introductory exercise draws on existing knowledge to outline the specific areas that psychologists have addressed within the concept of stress.

HOW DO YOU DO IT?

* Working in groups of five, complete the spidergrams provided on the next page. Brainstorm as many ideas as possible for each spidergram. Only refer to the textbook to check ideas you are unsure about.
* Points to discuss:
  Can you categorise the sources of stress you identified?
  Which sources of stress are beyond your control and which are not?
  Can you identify which of the physical and psychological effects of stress are short-term and which are long-term?

Notes

This activity can alternatively be addressed as a whole-class discussion, with summary spidergrams on the board.

Homework

Read and take notes from Gross, McIlveen *et al.* (2000), page 68, 'Defining stress'.

Ⓐctivity 32 Response sheet

Psychological
effects of
stress

Causes of
stress

Methods of
managing
stress

Methods of
measuring
stress

Physical
effects of
stress

ctivity 33 The physiological response to stress

Objective

To understand the physiology of the stress response.

Introduction

Our physiological response to stress involves two systems: the autonomic nervous system (ANS) and the endocrine system. The ANS is a self–regulating system, so it functions with little or no conscious control. It is the 'link' between the central nervous system and organs, glands and muscles of the intestines. The ANS has two branches with opposing functions. The sympathetic branch activates the internal organs and prepares the body to expend energy, the parasympathetic branch stimulates the processes that serve to conserve energy. The ANS achieves its effects via the endocrine system – this consists of ductless glands including the pituitary gland and the adrenal glands. Endocrine glands secrete hormones into the bloodstream which can have dramatic effects on our behaviour and emotions. In this activity a summary of the physiological stress response is completed.

HOW DO YOU DO IT?

- In pairs, complete the diagram on the next page. Use the words at the bottom of the page to fill in the blanks.
- Refer to Gross, McIlveen *et al.* (2000), page 69–72, if you need to.

Notes

This activity can be used as a revision task or a test task.

Homework

Read Gross, McIlveen *et al.* (2000), page 69, Box 4.1, and take notes to explain the function of the hypothalamus (50 words maximum).

Activity 33 Response sheet

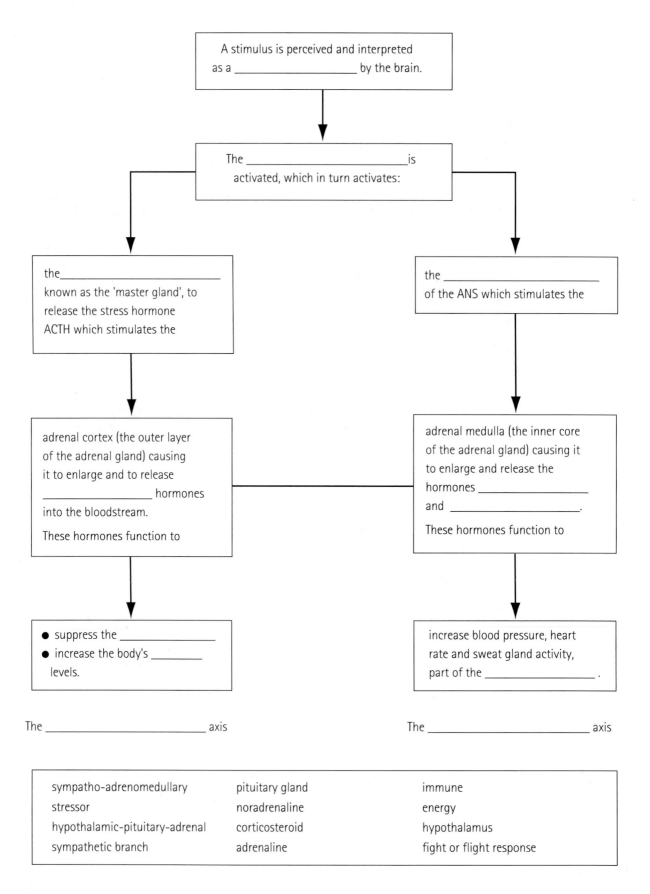

A stimulus is perceived and interpreted as a _____ by the brain.

The _____ is activated, which in turn activates:

the_____ known as the 'master gland', to release the stress hormone ACTH which stimulates the

the _____ of the ANS which stimulates the

adrenal cortex (the outer layer of the adrenal gland) causing it to enlarge and to release _____ hormones into the bloodstream.

These hormones function to

adrenal medulla (the inner core of the adrenal gland) causing it to enlarge and release the hormones _____ and _____.

These hormones function to

● suppress the _____
● increase the body's _____ levels.

increase blood pressure, heart rate and sweat gland activity, part of the _____ .

The _____ axis

The _____ axis

sympatho-adrenomedullary	pituitary gland	immune
stressor	noradrenaline	energy
hypothalamic-pituitary-adrenal	corticosteroid	hypothalamus
sympathetic branch	adrenaline	fight or flight response

Activity 34 The General Adaptation Syndrome (Selye, 1936)

Objective

To describe and evaluate Selye's General Adaptation Syndrome (1936).

Introduction

Selye (1936) was researching sex hormones in rats when he discovered the same pattern of physiological responses occurred whether he injected them with ovary tissue, toxic fluids or exposed them to any other trauma. He researched this non-specific reaction further and found it occurred in response to any adverse conditions, including surgical trauma and electric shocks. Selye concluded that the body's response to stress is non-specific i.e. the body's response is the same irrespective of the particular stressor. If the stressor can be managed, then the body returns to its original state but repeated or prolonged exposure to the stressor results in tissue damage, increased susceptibility to disease or even death. Selye terms this non-specific response to stress the 'general adaptation syndrome' (GAS). In this exercise each stage of the general adaptation syndrome is described.

HOW DO YOU DO IT?

Work in pairs.

- Imagine you are just about to sit an extremely important exam paper and that you are very nervous. Think hard about your feelings at a moment such as this and how your body reacts. Turn to the picture of the person in 'Stage One' on the next page. Label the picture with all the physiological responses you can identify.
- Read Gross, McIlveen *et al.* (2000), page 71. Write the answers to the following questions in the same box.
  What triggers the alarm reaction?
  What occurs during the initial shock phase?
  What occurs during the countershock phase?
- Read Gross, McIlveen *et al.* (2000), page 70, Box 4.2. Go back to the picture and add an explanation of how each physiological change may help us defend ourselves or run away from a threatening situation.
- Read Gross, McIlveen *et al.* (2000), page 73. Write the answers to the following questions in the 'Stage Two' box.
  What occurs physiologically during this stage?
  Whilst the individual may appear to be defending itself against the stressor, what unobservable process is occurring?
- Read Gross and McIlveen *et al.*, (2000) page 73. Write the answers to the following questions in the 'Stage Three' box.
  What occurs during this stage if the stressor is removed?
  What occurs during this stage if the stressor is prolonged or repeated?
- To discuss:
  Why was the stress response useful to our ancestors?
  Why is the stress response inappropriate for most modern stressors?

Homework

Take notes to evaluate Selye's research from Gross, McIlveen *et al.* (2000), page 73. Include further ideas of your own (200 words maximum).

Website reference

http://www.stresstop.com/articles/article1.html
Read the article 'Fight or flight: the evolution of stress'.

Activity 34 Response sheet

Stage 1: the alarm reaction; 'fight or flight'

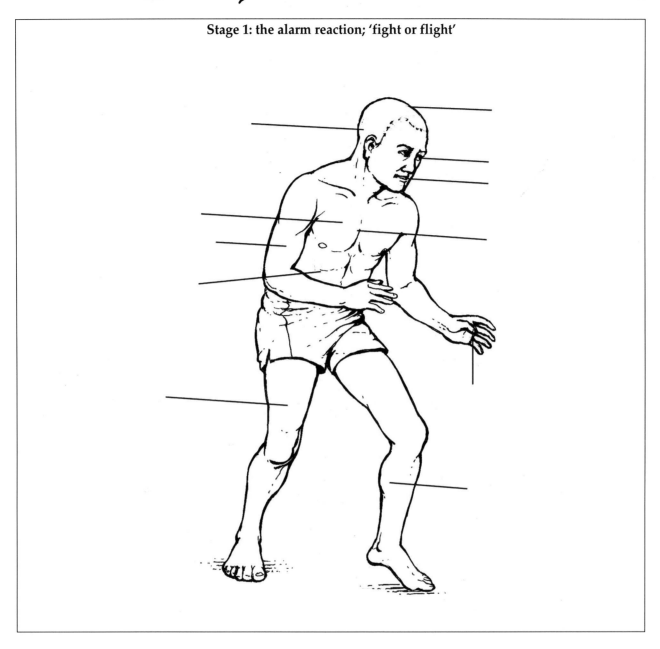

Stage 2: the resistance stage

Stage 3: the exhaustion stage

ctivity 35 Stress and the immune system

Objective

To summarise the effects of stress on the immune system.

Introduction

There is much evidence to suggest that stress impairs the functioning of the immune system and eventually causes illnesses. In this exercise a summary of the factors in this process is constructed.

HOW DO YOU DO IT?

- Working in pairs read through the half-sentences in the table on the next page.
- Draw arrows to match each half-sentence in the first column with the appropriate one in the second column.
- Read Gross, McIlveen *et al.* (2000), pages 74–76 'Stress and the immune system' and check your answers.

Notes

- Alternatively, this activity can be used as a revision exercise.
- Each completed summary sentence can be used as a starting point for further research and note-taking.

Homework

Describe and evaluate two research studies into the effects of stress on the immune system (200 words maximum).

Activity 35 **Response sheet**

Psychoneuroimmunology	production is lowered when the body is exposed to a stressor. This is a protein produced soon after tissue injury; it regulates the remodelling of connective tissue in wounds and the production of collagen, the tough fibrous tissues of scars. This is one way in which stress has a direct effect on the immune system.
The cells within the immune system are leucocytes (white blood cells)	suppress activity in the immune system.
Stressful life events have been linked to	function to seek, repel and destroy antigens (bacteria, viruses and other hazardous foreign bodies).
Corticosteroid	the study of psychological effects (including stress) on the immune system.
Interleukin-b	stress can affect the immune system indirectly by leading the individual to adopt an unhealthy lifestyle e.g. smoking and drinking.
Kiecolt-Glaser *et al.* (1995)	production increases when the body is exposed to a stressor. Intermittent production has negligible effects on the immune system but persistent production, as occurs in the GAS, impairs functioning by interfering with antibody production. This decreases and suppresses leucocyte activity. This is one way in which stress has a direct effect on the immune system.
Endorphins (the body's own natural painkillers, similar to morphine)	infectious illnesses including influenza, herpes and Epstein-Barr virus.
Marusic *et al.* (1999)	compared the rate of wound healing in a group of 'high stress' women, who were caring for relatives with Alzheimer's disease, with a 'stress-free' matched group. Complete wound healing typically took nine days longer in the 'high stress group'

Activity 36 A stress diary

Objective

To record and analyse a personal profile of stress.

Introduction

Keeping a stress diary is a good way of becoming aware of your own sources of stress, your reactions to stress and the everyday uplifts you experience that help to counteract the stressors.

HOW DO YOU DO IT?

You will need one week to gather the data for this activity. Working on your own, complete the following:

- Identify and make a list of your own reactions to stress (e.g. anger, headaches etc.).
- From the list choose the five symptoms most typical of how you feel when you are stressed and put them in the first column of Table 1 on the next page.
- At the end of each day enter in the table your stress score for each symptom, one indicating very little and ten indicating extreme experience of this symptom.
- In Table 2 each day identify the stressors that have occurred (e.g. train was delayed for 20 minutes) and also any uplifts (e.g. you enjoyed a game of football).
- At the end of the week plot a line graph of your stress symptoms using the axes over the page. Use a different coloured pen for each symptom. Complete the key.
- Discuss your findings in groups of three:
  Does your overall level of stress remain constant?
  Which are the most effective uplifts?
  Do different stressors produce different stress symptoms?
  If you kept a similar diary for another two weeks, would your three graphs be similar?
  What can you learn from this exercise about your own sources and levels of stress?

Notes

- You can also add up the scores for each symptom to give a stress score for the day. This can also be plotted on the line graph.
- A variation of this activity is to rate each stressor for its severity and each uplift for its effectiveness.

Activity 36 Response sheets

Table 1 Stress symptoms scores

Symptom	Monday	Tuesday	Wednesday	Thursday	Friday	Saturday	Sunday

Table 2 Stressors and uplifts

	Stressors/hassles	Uplifts
Monday		
Tuesday		
Wednesday		
Thursday		
Friday		
Saturday		
Sunday		

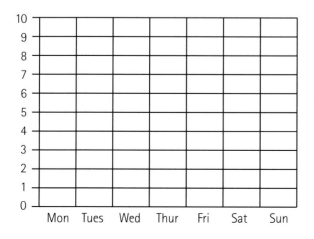

KEY

Symptom 1

Symptom 2

Symptom 3

Symptom 4

Symptom 5

Activity 37 **A case study of workplace stress**

Objective

To analyse an individual's experience of work-related stress.

Introduction

All jobs involve some stress but the sources and degree of stress vary. Not only can work stress result in physical and psychological effects for the individual, it can have profound consequences for employers. These include absenteeism, high staff turnover and poor performance in terms of quality and quantity of work. For these reasons companies are increasingly employing occupational psychologists to identify sources of stress in the workplace, both in terms of the work itself and the work environment. They also identify and give advice about appropriate methods of reducing stress.

HOW DO YOU DO IT?

In pairs, conduct an interview with one person you know in full-time employment. The interview will be semi-structured and your aim is to identify the sources of stress in that person's work-place and the effects of the stress the person experiences.
Note that this can be sensitive subject.

*   Design the open-ended questions that will form the basis of your interview. Carefully consider any relevant ethical issues, e.g. confidentiality.
    Areas to consider:
    – the physical environment including temperature, lighting, noise, space, etc.
    – transport to and from work
    – deadlines
    – workload
    – relations with colleagues
    – career progression
    – job security
    – clearly defined role
    – home/work interface
*   Record your interview.
*   Write a short report to summarise your findings, include an aim, method, results and evaluation. In the results section consider the following:
    Can the stressors identified by your interviewee be grouped into any categories?
    Are there any illustrative quotations you could include?
    In your evaluation include the advantages and disadvantages of using a semi-structured interview method.

Notes

*   This activity can be extended by pooling results between six pairs. Identify similarities and differences in the reports.
*   Can you compare your findings to the employment-related stressors identified by Hayward (1996), see Essential reading below.

Essential reading

Gross, McIlveen *et al.* (2000), page 81, Table 4.3 'Some effects of employment-related stressors', from Hayward (1996).

Website reference

http://mentalhealth.about.com/health/mentalhealth/gi/dynamic/offsite.htm?site=http://www.stress.org.uk/
This site focuses on personal and occupational stress management.

Activity 38 Stressful life events

Objective

To examine stressful live events particular to young people.

Introduction

The Social Readjustment Rating Scale was developed by Holmes & Rahe (1967) to demonstrate the link between stressful life events and health. They worked on the assumption that stress is created by any event that requires change. Based on their experiences as doctors they formed a list of life events that appeared to cluster in the months preceding the onset of illnesses in their patients. They gave 'marriage' an arbitrary value of 50 'life change' units. They then asked participants from a wide variety of backgrounds to assign a value to each of the other events according to the amount and intensity of readjustment they perceived them to require relative to getting married. The death of a spouse was considered the most stressful life event and was assigned a value of 100. From the scale Holmes and Rahe were then able to assess patients in terms of their state of health and the number of stressful life events they reported having experienced in the past year. They found that those who scored between 200 and 300 life change points in a given year had a 50% chance of developing health problems in the following year. Those scoring over 300 life change points had an 80% chance. However, one of the criticisms of this scale is that it is not relevant to young people. Young people experience many stressful life events, but these are not included in the scale. In this activity a scale more relevant to young people is developed and its limitations discussed.

HOW DO YOU DO IT?

- In groups of four, make a list of life events that you have experienced during the past year. This can be a sensitive subject so only mention events that you don't mind discussing.
- As a class, draw up a list of the twenty most common life events experienced by class members.
- Assign an arbitrary value of '50' to one life event on this final list.
- In your groups of four, assign a value to each of the other events according to the amount and intensity of stress you perceive them to cause relative to the event with a value of '50'.
- As a class, calculate the mean score assigned to each event and rank the events from most to least stressful.
- To discuss:
  Which events on the scale are positive changes and which are negative changes? Is Holmes and Rahe's assumption that all change is stressful necessarily true?
  What are the limitations of using a scale such as this one to assess the amount of stress a young person has experienced during the past year?
- Individually, write down a summary of your responses to the questions.

Notes

According to Kanner *et al.* (1981) it is the everyday events in life that are most stressful. These 'daily hassles' range from being stuck in a traffic jam to the pressures of deadlines at work. Read Gross, McIlveen *et al.* (2000), page 80, Box 4.8.

Homework

Take notes from Gross, McIlveen *et al.* (2000), pages 79–80, to evaluate the Holmes and Rahe Social readjustment rating scale (200 words maximum).

Activity 39 Gender differences in coping with stress

Objective

To discover whether men and women use different strategies to cope with stress in everyday life.

Introduction

Sources of stress are typically different for men and women. This is probably linked with traditional gender roles, with women taking most of the responsibility for child-care and men taking most of the responsibility for income. This activity is an investigation of whether men and women have different methods of dealing with stress.

HOW DO YOU DO IT?

- Working as a class, brainstorm as many ways of dealing with stress on an everyday level as you can think of (e.g. physical exercise).
- Agree a final list of twelve strategies.
- Now work in groups of three. Ask ten men and ten women to tick which three strategies they prefer as a way of unwinding after a stressful day.
- Write a summary of the aim, method, results and conclusion of your study. Include a bar graph to compare the strategies preferred by men and women.
- Questions to discuss:
  What is the most popular strategy overall?
  What is the most popular strategy for women? What is the most popular strategy for men?
  What differences, if any, can you see in the types of strategies men and women use?
  Which strategy do you think is the most effective – the most popular male or female choice?
  Why might men and women choose different methods for dealing with stress?

Notes

- A variation of this activity is to pool the data found by the different groups before writing up the results.
- A variation of this activity is to include investigating the different sources of stress for men and women. The participants can be asked to identify their three primary sources of stress either from a predetermined list or by responding freely. Can you relate these findings to the coping strategies preferred by each gender?

Homework

Take notes from Gross, McIlveen *et al.* (2000), pages 83–84 to outline the four explanations of why men have a higher mortality rate than women at every age. Use the following subheadings:

'Protective biological mechanism'
'Socialisation and gender roles'
'Type A/B personalities'
'Lifestyle differences'.

 Activity 40 Managing stress

Objective

To apply stress management techniques to case studies of stress.

Introduction

Each person's sources of stress, stress experience and way of coping with stress is unique to them. Because of the variety of both physical and psychological methods available to manage stress it is important that an individual finds a method appropriate to their needs. Often a person will have to try several methods before finding an effective strategy. In addition, successful stress management usually involves making some changes in lifestyle. In this exercise, three case studies of people suffering from stress are analysed and appropriate stress management techniques identified.

HOW DO YOU DO IT?

● Read the following case studies of three people suffering from stress.

The Journalist
Natasha is a journalist for a popular fashion magazine. In recent months her temper has been short, her patience has evaporated and she isn't sleeping properly. On top of it all she is beginning to lose interest in her job which has never happened before. She works long and irregular hours and each week has tight deadlines to meet. Her work day involves meetings, appointments and time at her desk in a very busy office. She has no break or lunch hour and tends to eat whenever she has a moment to grab a snack. She used to find her busy schedule a challenge but is now finding it increasingly difficult to keep up with her workload.

The Musician
Carl is a professional musician. Performing in front of an audience is exhausting and he also finds the travelling involved very tiring. However, sometimes there are slack periods during which he finds it difficult to keep motivated. Being self-employed he constantly worries about the lack of financial security and this concern has prevented him from pursuing new opportunities in his career. He had a shoulder injury recently which meant he couldn't work. He felt frustrated and depressed each time he had to turn down a performance. He does not feel that he has much control over his own life.

The Student
Anna is an AS level student. Recently she has begun to feel tired, anxious and irritable. She seems to have a permanent headache. Anna works part time in a supermarket for six hours each week but often works more hours at short notice to cover staff absences. She admits to being disorganised and only just manages to meet assignment deadlines, usually by working until the early hours of the morning. She is beginning to feel under pressure as module exams are looming. She is currently completing a coursework assignment but is unsure of the criteria as she missed the lesson it was set.

● For each case, identify practical measures the person could take to reduce the amount of stress in their life and suggest an appropriate physical or psychological method of managing stress. What are the reasons for your answers?
● Working individually, write a summary of your responses.

Notes

Are there any stress management techniques that would not be appropriate for each case study? Give reasons for your answers.

Homework

Compare and contrast one physical and one psychological method of managing stress (200 words maximum).

Essential reading

Read Gross, McIlveen *et al.* (2000), pages 85–90 'Stress management'.

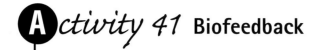

Activity 41 Biofeedback

Objective

To describe and evaluate biofeedback as a technique of stress management.

Introduction

Biofeedback is a physical method of managing stress based on laboratory procedures developed in the 1940s. These involved training research participants to gain some voluntary control over bodily functions that are not normally controlled voluntarily, such as blood pressure and heart rate. The term 'biofeedback' was coined in 1969, and refers to the individual using feedback from their own bodies as part of the process.

HOW DO YOU DO IT?

- Working in pairs access the following website: http://www.aapb.org/
  This is the website for the Association for Applied Physiology and Biofeedback.
- Answer the following questions:
  Describe the process of biofeedback as a method of stress management.
  Describe the equipment used in biofeedback.
  Which stress-related health problems can biofeedback help with?
  What are the advantages of using biofeedback as a method of stress management?
  Find evidence to support the effectiveness of biofeedback.

Notes

Both research and news on these websites are updated regularly. Look at these pages to see if there is any new research concerning biofeedback and stress.

Homework

Take notes to summarise the disadvantages of biofeedback as a method of stress management (Gross, McIlveen *et al.* (2000), page 86). Include any further ideas of your own.

Essential reading

Gross, McIlveen *et al.* (2000), pages 85–86 'Biofeedback'.

Activity 42 Revision exercise: Physical methods of stress management

Objective

To describe and evaluate physical methods of managing stress.

Introduction

This activity tests knowledge of physical methods of managing stress and reveals areas for further revision.

HOW DO YOU DO IT?

- Working in pairs, fill in as much of the diagram on the next page as you can, from memory.
- In a different coloured pen, use your class notes and textbook to complete the rest of the diagram.
- Consolidate your knowledge of the concepts you could not remember.

Notes

- A variation of this activity could be for half the group to use the diagram provided and half the group to construct their own revision diagram. It is useful to compare the completed work and discuss the benefits of different revision techniques.
- Construct a similar diagram for psychological methods of stress. Headings could include: relaxation and meditation, stress inoculation training, hardiness, strengths and weaknesses of each approach and a comparison to physical methods of managing stress.

Essential reading

Gross, McIlveen *et al.* (2000), pages 85–86, 'Physical approaches to managing the negative effects of stress'.

Activity 43 **Revision sheet**

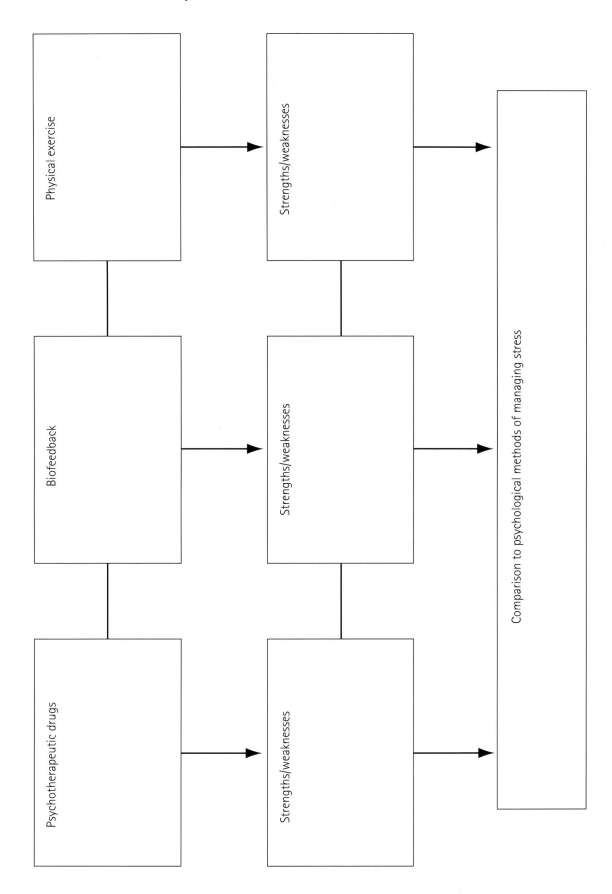

Physical methods of managing stress

Physical exercise

Biofeedback

Psychotherapeutic drugs

Strengths/weaknesses

Strengths/weaknesses

Strengths/weaknesses

Comparison to psychological methods of managing stress

Activity 43 The ten-minute meditation

Objective

To understand the nature of meditation and evaluate it as a method of managing stress.

Introduction

The aim of meditation is to reduce bodily arousal and it is therefore useful as a stress management technique. A meditation session usually lasts a minimum of twenty minutes, but this ten minute meditation is long enough to provide an example of the procedure and to realise the difficulties of the technique.

HOW DO YOU DO IT?

- The teacher should time this activity.
- Sit away from your desk with legs uncrossed and hands cupped one inside the other in your lap. Make sure you are comfortable.
- Close your eyes gently and begin to relax. Start with your feet and work upwards through your body, relaxing each muscle group.
- Breathe through your nose slowly and deeply, count each time you inhale. As you breathe count from one to ten, then start with one again.
- The object is to focus on breathing and counting and to exclude all other thoughts from your mind. When distracting thoughts occur try to push them out of your mind and focus again on breathing and counting.
- After ten minutes the teacher should ask the students to open their eyes and bring their thoughts back to the lesson.
- In groups of four discuss:
  Were you able to exclude other thoughts from your mind?
  What kind of thoughts interfered with your meditation? (e.g. worries and concerns.)
  What are the advantages and disadvantages of meditation as a method of managing stress?
- Individually complete the table on the next page. Include points from your group discussion and refer to Gross, McIlveen *et al.*, page 86, Box 4.15.

Notes

- Instead of focusing on counting, meditation often includes the individual repeating their mantra – a single sound or word.
- What are the differences between meditation and relaxation?

Homework

Compare and contrast meditation with two other stress management techniques you have studied (200 words maximum).

Websites

http://mentalhealth.about.com/health/mentalhealth/msub20.htm?mk=r2&terms=stress
This site focuses on various relaxation and meditation techniques as methods of stress management. It includes several online tutorials for you to try.

Activity *43* Response sheet

An evaluation of meditation as a stress management technique

Strengths	Weaknesses

Activity 44 Coping with stress

Objective

To understand Cohen & Lazarus' (1979) five categories of coping.

Introduction

Coping strategies involve behavioural and cognitive efforts to manage stressors. The type of coping strategy an individual adopts will influence whether they can manage and resist the effects of stress. Cohen & Lazarus (1979) have classified all the coping strategies a person might use into five general categories.

HOW DO YOU DO IT?

- The table on the next page has a summary of Cohen & Lazarus' (1979) classification of coping strategies. Working in pairs, complete the table with an example of a situation where you used each coping strategy.
- Review your completed table. Do you think the coping strategy you adopted was the most appropriate? Can you identify a coping strategy that would have been more effective?
- To discuss: Can an awareness of coping strategies help a person under stress?

Notes

The categories of coping strategies identified by Cohen and Lazarus can also be discussed in terms of primary and secondary control, Wade and Tavris (1993). Read Gross, McIlveen *et al.* (2000), page 89.

Homework

Take notes from Gross, McIlveen *et al.* (2000), page 90, to summarise how the five types of coping relate to Lazarus & Folkman's (1984) distinction between problem-focused and emotion-focused coping strategies. Under what circumstances are problem- and emotion-focused coping strategies appropriate? (100 words maximum.)

Website

http://www.uiuc.edu/departments/mckinley/health-info/stress/stress.html
Useful notes on both positive and negative coping strategies.

Activity 44 Response sheet

Cohen & Lazarus' (1979) five categories of coping strategies

Category	Strategy	Example
Direct action response	Trying to change or manipulate a relationship with the stressful situation (e.g. escaping from or removing it).	
Information seeking	Trying to understand the situation better and predict future situations related to the stressor.	
Inhibition of action	Doing nothing may be the best course of action if the situation is seen as short-term.	
Intrapsychic	Reappraising the situation by, for example, coping using psychological defence mechanisms, or changing the 'internal environment' (through, for example, drugs, relaxation or meditation).	
Turning to others	Using other people for help and emotional support.	

Activity 45 The perception of stressful events

Objective

To examine individual differences in the perception of stressful events.

Introduction

How we perceive a stressful event determines our experience of it. When an individual believes that an unpleasant event can be predicted, modified or terminated (in other words that they have some control over it) it is less likely to be perceived as stressful. There are individual differences in the way we perceive stress and in the coping strategies we use to try to manage it. In this exercise individual perceptions of the same stressful experience are compared and effective coping strategies identified.

HOW DO YOU DO IT?

- Working individually, write down eight stressful events you have experienced during the past year.
- Give each event a stress rating between one and ten, one indicating very little stress and ten extreme stress.
- In groups of four, identify the stressful events experienced that you have in common.
- Compare the ratings you gave these events.
- To discuss:
  Did people who found events less stressful perceive them differently or use different coping strategies? Points to consider in your discussion include:
  - whether the person adopted an internal or external locus of control (Gross, McIlveen *et al.,* 2000, page 89, Box 4.18)
  - whether the person adopted primary or secondary control (Gross, McIlveen *et al.,* (2000) page 89)
  - what type of coping strategy the person chose (Gross, McIlveen *et al.,* (2000) page 90, Table 4.4)
  - whether the event was perceived as a challenge or a burden.
- In your group, identify a stressful event that you will each experience in the future. Drawing on the conclusions from your previous discussion, how would this event best be dealt with?
- Individually, consider how different this approach would be from your usual way of dealing with a stressful event.

Notes

In the group discussion you can also compare 'internal dialogues'; see Gross, McIlveen *et al.* (2000), pages 86–87, 'Stress inoculation training'. Did people who experienced events as more stressful tend to engage in negative, self-defeating statements? (Note, this can be a sensitive issue.)

Homework

Read and take notes from Gross, McIlveen *et al.* (2000), pages 88–89. 'The role of control in the perception of stress'.

Activity 46 Revision summary: Stress

- Define the following terms:

      stress
      general adaptation syndrome.

- Describe one study (aim, method, results, conclusion) about each of the following:

      stress and the immune system
      stress and CHD
      life changes and stress
      the workplace and stress
      personality and stress
      gender and stress
      culture and stress.

- Describe and evaluate:

      one physical method of reducing stress
      one psychological method of reducing stress.

- Describe two studies which deal with the importance of 'control' in stress management.

Activity 47 **Multiple choice questions**

1 Who developed the social readjustment rating scale (SRRS) linking stressful life events to health problems?
 a Kahn & Cuthbertson (1998)
 b Holmes & Rahe (1967)
 c Kiecolt-Glaser *et al.* (1984)
 d Selye (1936).

2 Leucocytes form the basis of the cell population of the immune system and are known as:
 a white blood cells
 b antigens
 c corticosteroids
 d red blood cells.

3 Which of the following group of psychotherapeutic drugs are used to reduce the effects of stress:
 a antipsychotic drugs
 b antidepressant drugs
 c anti-inflammatory drugs
 d anxiolytic drugs.

4 Which of the following is NOT a stage of stress inoculation training:
 a application and follow-through
 b skill acquisition and rehearsal
 c self-evaluation
 d cognitive preparation.

5 The sympathetic branch of the autonomic nervous system prepares the body to:
 a expend energy
 b conserve energy
 c suppress the immune system
 d release hormones.

6 Primary control involves:
 a an individual trying to accommodate to reality by changing his/her own perceptions, goals and desires
 b an individual having a false perception of control
 c an individual trying to influence existing reality by changing other people, events or circumstances
 d an individual having a high internal locus of control.

7 In the resistance stage of the GAS:
 a the immune system is less responsive to infection or physical change
 b the individual's pupils dilate
 c the body's resources are being depleted
 d both a and c.

8 Type A individuals tend to be:
 a relaxed, easy going and calm
 b less stressed than Type B individuals
 c ambitious, competitive, perfectionists
 d none of the above.

9 One criticism of the SRRS is that:
   a research with the SRRS is correlational rather than experimental
   b research with the SRRS is experimental rather than correlational
   c the scale includes events that can occur only once
   d the scale is time consuming to complete.

10 Acculturative stress refers to:
   a racism
   b the emotional challenge faced by African-Americans of living in a majority white community with different values and beliefs
   c daily hassles
   d stress in the workplace.

11 Biofeedback:
   a allows the individual to bring autonomic functions under voluntary control
   b enables the individual to control his/her anger and frustration
   c is part of the process of meditation
   d allows the individual to identify his/her sources of stress.

12 Which of the following stressful events does not appear in the SRRS:
   a retirement
   b pregnancy
   c examinations
   d begin or end school.

13 The stress response originates in the:
   a hypothalamus
   b pons
   c medulla
   d cerebellum.

14 According to Kobasa (1986) 'hardy' individuals:
   a view change as a challenge and perceive themselves as having a high degree of control
   b tend to have more stress-related illnesses
   c are hard-driving and competitive
   d are easy-going and relaxed.

15 A drawback of meditation as a method of stress management is that:
   a there are possible side-effects
   b it takes time and space
   c it requires a therapist
   d it cannot be used in conjunction with other methods.

16 Problem-focused coping strategies (Lazarus & Folkman, 1984) involve:
   a devising and adhering to a plan to deal with a stressor
   b using others for emotional support
   c avoiding the stressor
   d learning to live with the stressor.

17 Glass & Singer (1972) in their laboratory study of noise as a stressor concluded:
   a noise is not a stressor
   b mere knowledge that there is control over a stressor is sufficient to reduce stress
   c it makes no difference if a person feels s/he has control over a stressor
   d having control increases our level of stress.

18 Kiecolt-Glaser *et al.* (1995) compared rate of wound healing in a group of 'high stress' women compared to a 'stress-free' matched group. They found:

   a wound healing took on average nine days longer in the stress-free group

   b wound healing took the same amount of time in both groups

   c wound healing took one day longer in the high stress group

   d wound healing took nine days longer in the high stress group.

19 Meichenbaum's (1976) SIT assumes that people sometimes find situations stressful because:

   a of their misinterpretations about them

   b they are physically unfit

   c they do not take time out to relax

   d they adopt primary control.

20 According to Kanner *et al.* (1981) 'daily hassles':

   a are more influential as stressors than life changes

   b are less influential as stressors than life changes

   c have no effect on our overall experience of stress

   d require further research as a source of stress.

Answers to Activity 47

 1 b
 2 a
 3 d
 4 c
 5 a
 6 c
 7 d
 8 c
 9 a
10 b
11 a
12 c
13 a
14 a
15 b
16 a
17 b
18 d
19 a
20 a

4

Individual Differences: Abnormality

Specification topic	Gross, McIlveen et al. (2000) 2nd edition	Activity	Page
Defining psychological abnormality	93–100		
• In terms of statistical infrequency, deviation from social norms, a 'failure to function adequately' and deviation from ideal mental health	94–100	48 Defining psychological abnormality 49 Describe and evaluate psychological definitions of abnormality	88 89
• Limitations of these definitions (including cultural relativism)	94–100	50 Problems in defining normality and abnormality across different cultures	91
Biological and psychological models of abnormality	**100–107**	51 Assumptions of psychological models of abnormality and their implications for treatment	92
• Assumptions of biological (medical) model and implications for treatment	100–101	52 An evaluation of the concept of mental illness 53 Gender bias in mental health 54 Some are more equal than others! Women and mental health 55 Labelling as a product of the medical model	93 94 95 96
• Assumptions of psychodynamic model and implications for treatment	101–103		
• Assumptions of behavioural model and implications for treatment	103–104	56 A study to investigate the relationship between fear and experienced trauma	97
• Assumptions of cognitive model and implications for treatment	104–105	57 Assumptions of the cognitive model of abnormality – rational and irrational thought processes 58 Behavioural and cognitive models: the implications for treatment	99 100
Eating disorders – anorexia nervosa and bulimia nervosa	**107–112**		
• Clinical characteristics of anorexia nervosa • Explanations and research studies on anorexia nervosa • Clinical characteristics of bulimia nervosa • Explanations and research studies on bulimia nervosa		59 Media portrayals of the ideal female form 60 An investigation into the effect of pre-adolescent role models and the development of eating disorders 61 Men and eating disorders: the forgotten minority 62 Revision summary: eating disorders 63 Revision summary sheet: individual differences 64 Multiple choice questions	101 103 105 106 108 109

General textbook:

Gross, R., McIlveen, R., *et al.* (2000) *Psychology: A New Introduction for A Level*

Activity 48 Defining psychological abnormality

Objective

To identify criteria for defining normal and abnormal behaviour.

Introduction

The concept of abnormality is an extremely difficult one to define precisely. The aim of this activity is to explore the concepts of normality and abnormality, to experience at first hand the problems in defining precisely normal and abnormal behaviour.

Materials

Stimulus materials: a set of photographs of famous people to start the discussions (e.g. Albert Einstein, Calista Flockhart, Carl Lewis, Linford Christie, Sharon Stone and Marilyn Monroe). Overhead acetates and acetate pens.

HOW DO YOU DO IT?

- Working in groups of three or four make a list of the characteristics which best describe an individual whose behaviour you consider to be normal.
  Why do you consider this behaviour to be 'normal'? Justify your list of characteristics.
- How do you think abnormal behaviour differs from the normal behaviours that you have previously listed?
  Use the stimulus material provided; think about whether these famous individuals are abnormal in any way.
- What criteria would you use to define a person as abnormal?
- Write down your responses to these questions on the acetates provided and be ready to discuss your views with the whole class. It will be interesting to see to what extent the groups agree or disagree on the criteria for normal and abnormal behaviour.

Notes

- This activity should demonstrate the difficulty in arriving at a universally acceptable definition of abnormality.
- Many researchers, including Szasz (1960) and Rosenhan & Seligman (1989), believe that the difficulty stems from the fact that abnormality is an imprecise and subjective concept.

Websites

http://www.mind.org.uk
This is the official website of MIND, a mental health charity for England and Wales.

Activity 49 Describe and evaluate psychological definitions of abnormality

Objectives

- To define abnormality in terms of statistical infrequency, deviation from social norms, a 'failure to function adequately', and deviation from ideal mental health.
- To identify the limitations associated with these psychological definitions of abnormality.

Introduction

Although it can be seen from the previous activity that normality and abnormality are difficult concepts to define, psychologists have, nonetheless, attempted a number of definitions of abnormality. See what you think of them!

HOW DO YOU DO IT?

Complete the table on the next page.
Make sure that you address the following psychological definitions of abnormality:

- abnormality as 'statistical infrequency'
- abnormality as 'deviation from ideal mental health'
- abnormality as a 'failure to function adequately'
- abnormality as a 'deviation from social norms'.

You will need to read pages 93–99 in Gross, McIlveen *et al.* (2000) to complete this table fully.

Notes

Completing the table in this way should help with revision.

Website reference

http://www.scar.utoronto.ca/~zakzanis/psyb32/Lecture1/v3_document.htm
This website gives a clear account of the various definitions of abnormality.

Activity 49 Response sheet

Definition of abnormality	Explanation of abnormal behaviour	Limitations of definition

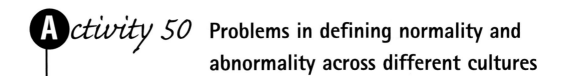

Activity 50 Problems in defining normality and abnormality across different cultures

Objective

To take into account cultural relativism in defining abnormality.

Introduction

One of the major problems with psychological definitions of abnormality is that they do not take into account differences between cultures. The concept of cultural relativism means that value judgements are relative to individual cultural context and we cannot make absolute statements about what is normal or abnormal in human behaviour. The implication of this is that different cultures will have different criteria as to what constitutes normality and abnormality. This accepted, it is almost impossible to arrive at a universally agreed definition of abnormality. Behaviour regarded as deviant or dysfunctional in one culture may be quite acceptable in another. Some syndromes are regarded as 'culture bound syndromes' (CBSs) which means that they may be present in some cultures but not others.

HOW DO YOU DO IT?

- Think of a behaviour that is considered normal in one culture but not in another.
- Think of behaviours which were considered abnormal 50–100 years ago, but today are accepted by society as normal.
- Think of one behaviour in our culture which was thought normal 50–100 years ago but would now be regarded as abnormal.
- Examples of culture bound syndromes include anorexia nervosa and bulimia nervosa. There is a high incidence of these eating disorders in Western industrialised societies. Write down as many reasons as you can which may explain the high incidence of anorexia nervosa and bulimia nervosa in Western cultures such as the USA and Western Europe.

Notes

This activity introduces the concept of cultural relativism and the notion that definitions of abnormality fail to taken into account cultural differences. Students should understand that definitions of abnormality differ between cultures, so what is considered as abnormal in one culture may be considered normal in another. In addition, definitions of abnormality may differ over periods of time.

Homework

Attempts to define psychological abnormality have failed to take account of cultural differences. Discuss (300 words maximum).

Essential reading

Gross, McIlveen *et al.* (2000), pages 93–101.

Activity 51 Assumptions of psychological models of abnormality and their implications for treatment

Objective

To consider psychological models of abnormality including their assumptions regarding abnormal behaviour, their implications for treatment and a brief evaluation.

Introduction

Psychological models which need to be considered: the psychoanalytic model, the behaviourist model and the cognitive model. A sound knowledge of these psychological models will be useful in looking at eating disorders. Each model has a set of assumptions regarding the cause of abnormal behaviour, and as a result this has a number of implications for the treatment of abnormal behaviour.

Materials

A3 poster paper.

HOW DO YOU DO IT?

The class must be divided into four groups. Each group will have responsibility for producing a poster summarising one model of abnormality from the list below:

- Biological (medical) model
- Psychodynamic model
- Behavioural model
- Cognitive model.

On the poster, you need to include details of the following:

- key assumptions regarding the cause of abnormal behaviour
- key techniques for the treatment of abnormal behaviour
- a brief evaluation.

Make the posters as interesting as you can – be creative. There may be a prize for the best poster in the class!
You will, as a group, present your poster and its content to the whole class.

Notes

This activity should provide useful summaries of the models of abnormality covered by the AS specification. The most useful will be clear and concise; the use of keywords and bullet points should help.

Homework

Outline the major causes of abnormal behaviour according to any two models of abnormality (300 words maximum).

Essential reading

Gross, McIlveen *et al.* (2000), pages 101–105.

Activity 52 An evaluation of the concept of mental illness

Objective

To understand the problems associated with the term mental illness.

Introduction

According to Scheff (1970) 'the term "mental illness" and its associated concepts, "symptoms", "diagnosis", "therapy" and "patient" – is a product of the medical model'. A critical assumption of the medical model is that abnormal behaviour may be likened to a disease. The model draws an analogy between physical disease and mental illness. However, this model has been criticised for adopting the so-called 'sickness analogy' by a number of 'anti-psychiatrists'.

HOW DO YOU DO IT?

Thomas Szasz, one of the most outspoken 'anti-psychiatrists' holds controversial views on the concept of mental illness. Thomas Szasz' opinions are clear when you consider the titles of his books which include *The Myth of Mental Illness* and *The Manufacture of Madness*.
Working in groups, discuss the meaning and implications of the following quotations from *The Manufacture of Madness*:

- '... the concept of mental illness is analogous to that of witchcraft' (page 19)
- '... the concept of mental illness serves the same social function in the modern world as did the concept of witchcraft in the late Middle Ages...' (page 19)
- '... witchcraft and mental illness are imprecise and all-encompassing concepts, freely adaptable to whatever uses the priest or physician wishes to put to them...' (page 19)
- '... in the past, men created witches; now they create mental patients...' (page 20)

To have a meaningful discussion you will need to find out about 'witches' and how they were treated during the Middle Ages. Think about how the plight of the 'witches' during the Middle Ages is similar to the plight of the mentally ill today. Make sure that you take and keep notes of your discussion for revision purposes.
Read Box 5.5 'The "demonological" model of abnormality' on page 100 of Gross, McIlveen *et al.* (2000).

Notes

- Thomas Szasz saw the term mental illness as a form of social control. He claims that many mental disorders have no known physical cause, yet are labelled as mental illness on the subjective judgement of the psychiatrist simply because they do not conform to the norms. In the same way as the term 'witch' was applied to individuals whose religious beliefs and practices deviated from the norm in the Middle Ages, today, the term 'mental illness' is often applied to those whose behaviour differs from that of the majority.
- Szasz also argues that there are no scientifically precise ways of deciding what kinds of beliefs or behaviours are socially healthy, in a way which is equivalent to the definition of physical health.

Activity 53 Gender bias in mental health

Objective

To understand the meaning of gender-role stereotyping and how it may influence mental health.

Introduction

The medical model assumes a universal standard of mental health, which tends to be based on the white, middle-class European male. Differences in education, sex and race mean that some individuals are more likely to have their symptoms labelled as abnormal or to be labelled as mentally ill, than are others.

According to research, clinical judgements of women have tended to reflect the traditional stereotype of femininity centred on passivity, dependency and 'putting others before oneself'; characteristics which are contrary to healthy adult behaviour, which is centred on activity, independence and assertiveness.

HOW DO YOU DO IT?

Ask participants to tell you or write down the characteristics of the following:
- a mentally healthy male
- a mentally healthy female
- a mentally healthy adult.

Some examples of characteristics may include: emotional, assertive, passive.

Decisions to make.
- Will you ask each participant to identify the characteristics of all three?
- Will you ask a different group of participants to identify the characteristics of each?
  In making this decision you may want to think about which method would give the most reliable results.
- Will you give your participants a list of characteristics to choose from?
- Will you leave it up to each participant to choose the characteristics which they believe are the most suitable?

Analysis of findings
Look for common characteristics for the mentally healthy male, mentally healthy female and mentally healthy adult. You may want to construct a tally chart to show the number of times a particular characteristic is used for each, as shown below:

Characteristic	Mentally healthy male	Mentally healthy female	Mentally healthy adult
Assertiveness			

Notes

- Broverman *et al.* (1981) state that since certain behavioural characteristics have traditionally been ascribed to either male or female genders, it is likely that clinical diagnosis of mental disorders will reflect these distinctions.
- Broverman *et al.* (1981) also asked 46 male and 33 female mental health professionals to rate the characteristics of the healthy man, woman and adult. They found that the healthy adult and healthy man were rated in a similar way (assertive, decisive and independent); the healthy woman was viewed as submissive, dependent and emotional.

Activity 54 Some are more equal than others! Women and mental health

Objective

To identify factors that contribute to the fact that a woman is twice as likely as a man to be diagnosed as suffering from depression.

Introduction

The assumption is that the medical model is based on a universal standard of mental health which reflects the white, middle-class male. This itself suggests why women are over-represented in the statistics for depression.

HOW DO YOU DO IT?

Working in groups of three to four, identify factors which may explain why women are twice as likely as men to be diagnosed as suffering from depression. You will want to take into account Broverman *et al.*'s (1981) research on gender-role stereotyping by mental health professionals. They found that the healthy adult and healthy man were rated in a similar way – assertive, decisive and independent. The healthy woman was viewed as submissive, dependent and emotional. How might this view, if held by mental health professionals, contribute to the over-representation of women in the statistics for depression?

Finally, think about how the stereotype of a healthy man and the traditional male stereotype may contribute to the fact that men are less likely than women to be diagnosed as suffering from depression. Make notes on your findings.

Notes

The issue here concerns bias in the diagnostic process, based as it is on assumptions made by medical professionals on traditional male and female stereotypes. Cochrane (1995) explains the over-representation of women as being due to five factors:

1 prevalence not reflecting true prevalence
2 biological factors
3 long-term effects of child abuse
4 gender-role socialisation
5 depression as a coping strategy for women.

Activity 55 Labelling as a product of the medical model

Objective

To understand the concept of labelling as a product of the medical model.

Introduction

Individuals who are diagnosed as mentally ill carry with them a stigma, which will affect them for the rest of their lives. Scheff (1966) explains that the mentally ill person is seen as breaking a set of 'residual rules' of society, which are rather vague and unspecified and do with 'decency' and 'reality'. For those observing, the strange and frightening behaviour results in labelling (primary deviation). Once society can no longer tolerate the unusual behaviour of an individual, the psychiatrist, acting on behalf of society labels him/her as 'ill', after fitting him/her into a neat category using the medical model. Labelling, in turn, affects the individual and may then lead to additional behaviour, characteristic of the mentally ill (self-fulfilling prophecy).

Materials

A copy of the video *One Flew Over the Cuckoo's Nest* (Certificate 18).

HOW DO YOU DO IT?

Read the following questions before watching *One Flew Over the Cuckoo's Nest*. These questions will form the basis of a class discussion, but must be written up afterwards.

Background
McMurphy (Jack Nicholson) is accused of rape, but rather than facing the prospect of going to prison, he pretends to be mentally ill, and is sent for observation at a mental institution. Sister Ratchet is in charge of the ward.

- Why are McMurphy and his friends in the institution?
- Identify the ways in which the lives of the inmates are controlled.
- How was drug time organised?
- What does the incident regarding the World Series Baseball suggest about the control at the institution and why did this incident cause such a problem?
- What did the fishing trip reveal about the inmates?
- What does the outburst caused by the cigarette end landing in an inmate's trousers and burning him suggest about labelling?
- What leads to the change in 'The Chief's' behaviour?
- How and why does McMurphy's behaviour change throughout the film?

Notes:

- *One Flew Over the Cuckoo's Nest* is Certificate 18 and does contain some rather 'colourful' language.
- In this film many of the patients in the hospital responded to their label and defined themselves as mentally ill. Until the arrival of McMurphy they passively conform to the roles expected of the mental patient, behaving in accordance with the diagnosis and label that had been applied to their 'illness'. This film clearly demonstrates the effect of institutionalisation and the impact of being confined, with little stimulation, and how this may contribute to abnormal behaviour.

Activity 56 **A study to investigate the relationship between fear and experienced trauma**

Objective

To establish the validity of the behaviourists' claim that abnormal behaviour is the result of faulty learning.

Introduction

The behaviourist approach interprets abnormal behaviour in terms of faulty learning. Like all behaviours, abnormal behaviour is acquired through a process of conditioning. Of central importance is the behaviourists' claim that behaviour is largely determined by the environment. They argue that the reason why people behave in different ways is because they have been exposed to different environments and so have had different learning experiences.

Behaviourists have explained the development of phobias (irrational fears of objects, situations or events, characterised by avoidance of that object, situation or event) by the process of classical conditioning. An individual may develop a phobia when a neutral stimulus (one that doesn't naturally elicit a fearful response) is paired with a frightening event. The aim of this study is for students to investigate the extent to which there is a relationship between fear and trauma. If the behaviourist claim is accurate then the prediction would be that there is a positive correlation between fear and trauma.

HOW DO YOU DO IT?

This will involve a correlational analysis, which investigates the relationship between covariables: fear and experienced trauma.
You will need to design a questionnaire.

- Choose a number of events, objects or situations e.g. open spaces, enclosed spaces, crowds, spiders, snakes, illness, lifts, exams.
- You will need to ask your respondents to rate each of these in terms of the extent to which the objects, events or situations listed trigger feelings of anxiety, panic or fear.
- Choose an appropriate scale, for example: '1= no feelings of fear, would not avoid the event, object or situation', to '3 = distinct feelings of anxiety/panic, would try hard to avoid such an event, object or situation'.
- Then you will need to ask each respondent to indicate to what extent he or she has personally experienced a trauma with regard to the event, object or situation listed. Again, you will need to choose an appropriate scale for example: '1 = experienced no trauma' to '3 = experience a traumatic event'.

Your questionnaire should look something like this:

Event, object, situation	Fear rating (1, 2 or 3)	Trauma rating (1, 2 or 3)
Open spaces		
Enclosed spaces		
Spiders		

You need to write some instructions for your respondents. Do not forget to take into account ethical issues (e.g. how will you make sure that none of your respondents will be upset by this questionnaire?) You may want to pilot your questionnaire first. You then need to identify your sampling procedure before you collect your own data.

Analysing the results:
Once you have collected all the data you need to work out the mean fear score and mean trauma score for each object, situation and event.

Event, object, situation	Fear rating (1, 2 or 3)	Trauma rating (1, 2 or 3)
Open spaces	2.4	2.5
Enclosed spaces	1.4	1.6

You can then plot a scattergram to establish the strength of the relationship between fear and trauma.

Homework

Read and make notes on pages 103–104 of Gross, McIlveen *et al.* (2000) to consolidate your knowledge.

Activity 57 Assumptions of the cognitive model of abnormality – rational and irrational thought processes

Objective

To identify some common irrational/undesirable and rational/desirable thoughts.

Introduction

The cognitive model suggests that faulty thinking processes produce abnormal behaviour. This approach sees the individual as an active processor of information, and it is the way in which individuals perceive, anticipate and evaluate events, rather than the events themselves, which have the greatest impact on behaviour.

According to Ellis (1958) an 'activating event' triggers a highly charged, emotion/feeling which, in turn, has consequences for an individual's behaviour. According to the cognitive model, individuals may respond in rational and irrational ways to activating events. It is the irrational responses which may lead to abnormal behaviour. For example, suppose an individual fails his/her psychology test. A rational response might include acknowledgement that the last minute revision was insufficient, but next time, with more thorough revision, the situation should improve. An irrational response would involve the individual believing that failure in the psychology test meant that he/she was stupid and useless, leading to him/her dropping out of the course.

HOW DO YOU DO IT?

Think about the following 'activating event'.
You have arranged to meet your boyfriend/girlfriend at the cinema. He/she fails to turn up and you wait outside the cinema for an hour before giving up and going home. Complete the model below:

Rational/desirable	Irrational/undesirable
Thoughts/beliefs regarding the activating event	
Emotions regarding the activating event	
Behavioural consequences	

What are the implications of this approach for the treatment of abnormal behaviour?

Notes

According to this model, irrational thoughts lead to depression, a disorder characterised by the sufferer having persistent negative thoughts.

Homework

Read Box 5.10 in 'Therapies based on the cognitive model' from Gross, McIlveen *et al.* (2000) and make brief notes.

Activity 58 Behavioural and cognitive models: the implications for treatment

Objective

To understand the application of the behaviourist and cognitive models in the treatment of abnormal behaviour.

Introduction

Behavioural approaches to depression focus on the role played by reinforcement. A depressed person may spend less time in social activities, which initially leads to concern and attention being paid by that person's friends. Behaviourists argue that the attention the depressed person receives reinforces the depressed behaviour. Researchers have found that depressed people report having fewer pleasant experiences than non-depressed people, and that greater depression is correlated with fewer pleasant experiences. As abnormal behaviour is caused by faulty learning through inappropriate reinforcement, the aim of behaviour therapy is to reinforce the normal or desired behaviour, whilst making sure that the abnormal behaviour is not reinforced, and is therefore extinguished.

On the other hand, those adopting the cognitive model believe that depression is based on self-defeating negative thoughts and irrational beliefs. Abnormal behaviour results from faulty thinking; therefore, the aim of cognitive therapy is to challenge these irrational beliefs and negative thoughts.

HOW DO YOU DO IT?

Case study: Clinical depression

Adam is a thirty-year-old solicitor who is suffering from depression. His mood is continuously sad and depressed, he feels low from the moment he wakes up in the morning to the time he goes to bed. He is having great difficult in sleeping, although he constantly feels tired. He used to be an active individual playing squash, two or three times a week. However his lack of energy and constant lethargy means that he no longer engages in any activity. Activities that used to provide him with great pleasure in the past no longer do. In addition, he is finding it increasingly difficult to focus on his work, he no longer feels that he can concentrate on legal cases, and his boss has already received several complaints about him failing to meet deadlines. He feels as if life is a drag and utterly useless.

The class should be divided into two groups. One group should prepare a behavioural therapy programme for Adam, whilst the other prepares a cognitive therapy programme. Each group must include a detailed explanation of which techniques they have adopted from each model, as well as an account of why the proposed therapy programme will be successful.

Read Gross, McIlveen *et al.* (2000), pages 104–105 to help with your decisions.
Make notes and summarise your main points on an acetate. You will be expected to give a presentation of your therapy programme to the whole class.

Notes

One would expect those preparing a behavioural therapy programme to focus on behaviour modification techniques, such as token economy programmes, whilst those preparing a cognitive therapy programme are likely to focus on the work of Beck & Weishaar (1989).

Activity 59 Media portrayals of the ideal female form

Objective

To identify ways in which Western magazines portray women.

Introduction

One explanation for anorexia nervosa (AN) comes from the behavioural model, which suggests that AN is the result of the impact of social norms, values and roles. AN is specific to the USA and Western Europe; it is not found in any other culture (culture-bound syndrome) and it may therefore be assumed that the social norms, values and roles of the USA and Western Europe may contribute to the high incidence of AN. Everyday the media presents individuals with 'idealised images' of the human form. The majority of AN sufferers are white, middle-class, young women. Men only represent 5–10 per cent of all cases. Magazines aimed at teenagers contain photographs of 'supermodels' representing the 'ideal' human form, for example, Kate Moss, Christie Turlington, Elle Macpherson, Naomi Campbell and Jodie Kidd.

Materials

Glossy magazines aimed at teenagers.

HOW DO YOU DO IT?

- Collect as many magazines as you can. Count the number of times a 'supermodel' (e.g. tall, thin, very long legs) is shown in the magazines, and compare with the number of times a picture of an 'average' woman (e.g. size 14–16) is shown. Before you start this exercise on content analysis, you will need to operationalise your definitions of 'supermodels' and 'average women'.
- Use the information you gather to complete the grid on the next page.
- Write up your conclusions and suggest the implications of your findings.

Notes

The findings should reveal a very low frequency of 'average' women and a high frequency of 'supermodels'. Think about the types of images teenage girls are exposed to, and how this may affect their perceptions of their own bodies.

Homework

Read Gross, McIlveen *et al.* (2000), page 110 to consolidate your knowledge.

Webpages:

http://www.edauk.com
The Eating Disorders Association has a useful website on anorexia nervosa and bulimia nervosa. It provides in-depth information in a very readable format.
http://rcpsych.ac.uk/public/help/anor/anor-frame.htm
The website of the Royal College of Psychiatrists provides clear and accurate information on eating disorders.
http://www.bbc.co.uk/health/features/eating-disorders.shtml
The BBC's website on eating disorders.

Activity 59 Response sheet

Name of magazine	Frequency of portrayal of 'supermodel types'	Frequency of portrayal of 'average women'

Activity 60 An investigation into the effect of pre-adolescent role models and the development of eating disorders

Objective

To investigate the effect of pre-adolescent role models on the development of eating disorders.

Introduction

It is not only women's fashion magazines which may play an important role in providing role models for young girls. According to Dr Andrew Hill, 'girls of eight are obsessed with body shape and take their lead from the changing figure of Sindy dolls'. He believes that Sindy who is now 'unashamedly blonde, pointedly thin, dressed immaculately, with a lifestyle to match', is usually bought for girls in the six to eight-year-old age group.

HOW DO YOU DO IT?

Read the following article from page 8 of *The Times*, 14th September 1996.

Sindy blamed for girls' weight fears

Girls as young as eight or nine are worried about their weight and many are dieting though they are not overweight. Dr Andrew Hill of Leeds University told the meeting that the pressure to be thin, reinforced by magazines, television and even the changing shapes of dolls, was already well-developed in pre-adolescent girls.

Sindy dolls provided one example of the pressures. 'Originally manufactured in the early 1960s as a toy for young teenage girls, thirty-something Sindy has lost her brunette bob, plain clothes and doll-like shape,' he said. 'She is now unashamedly blonde, pointedly thin, dressed immaculately with a lifestyle to match, and bought for the six, seven or eight-year-old girl. Not only does 90s Sindy depict the ideal appearance and lifestyle of the 90s woman, she does so for girls only halfway to puberty.'

Dr Hill questioned 176 eight-year-olds, offering them images of different body shapes to discover how they perceived their bodies and whether they were aware of dieting. The girls consistently picked a body shape thinner than their own and those who were especially aware of dieting had the lowest self-esteem.

Similar tests with nine-year-olds produced the same results, with 41 per cent placing their preferred body shape at a point thinner than their own. When boys were asked the same questions, the opposite result emerged. Among nine-year-olds 41 per cent placed wanted to be broader, with 28 per cent choosing a thinner shape. The worrying aspect of the girls' perception, he said, was that it lay in the opposite direction to their impending physical development.

Sarah Howard, public relations manager for Hasbro, which manufactures Sindy, said 'Why pick on Sindy?' Young girls spend only a small amount of time playing with the dolls. 'An 11½ inch piece of plastic is not responsible for the ills of today's society.'

'As a responsible toy and game manufacturer we have to make our products move with the times. We have done a lot of research with parents and they know what they want from fashion dolls.'

The class should be divided into two groups. One group will present an argument supporting Dr Andrew Hill's view that Sindy is to blame for girls' weight fears, whilst the other group will present an argument against Dr Hill's view. Each group must prepare their arguments, and questions which they propose to ask the opposing side. They must then nominate two speakers who will present each argument to the class.

Notes

- Those arguing in favour of Dr Hill's point of view should consider evidence such as the fact that females outnumber males in the statistics for eating disorders. Although the onset is during adolescence, onset may sometimes occur before adolescence, for example, Lask & Bryant-Waugh (1992) have reported cases in children as young as eight. Other evidence which may be used can be found in Gross, McIlveen *et al.* (2000), pages 110–111.
- Those arguing against Dr Hill's point of view should focus on the reliability and validity of the research evidence (this can be linked to the work covered in the research methods module (AS Module 3)). Points for discussion should include problems with the use of correlational analysis and the difficulty in establishing a cause–effect relationship. This group should also look at alternative explanations and consider their validity.

Activity 61 Men and eating disorders: the forgotten minority

Objective

To consider the prevalence of anorexia nervosa and bulimia nervosa in men.

Introduction

According to Ian Murray, Medical Correspondent for *The Times* 'Men are "forgotten" anorexics'. In an article which appeared on 15/08/99 he states that men make up to ten per cent of the 60,000 people diagnosed with illnesses such as anorexia and bulimia.

HOW DO YOU DO IT?

Although men make up ten per cent of the 60,000 people suffering from anorexia and bulimia, the Eating Disorders Association believes that the figure for sufferers is much higher and is on the increase.

Working in small groups, identify as many reasons as you can to explain why the Eating Disorders Association believes that men are under-represented in the statistics for anorexia nervosa and bulimia nervosa.

Notes

Issues raised in Ian Murray's article include the following:
- failure of doctors to recognise the symptoms
- men are less likely to admit having a problem
- symptoms will obviously be different, making it more difficult for doctors to detect the warning signs
- doctors and psychologists are not used to seeing men and may not pick up on the warning signs that they are suffering from an eating disorder
- men tend not to starve themselves, but rather overexercise and cut down on the amount they eat
- men may not appear emaciated, but instead appear muscular, yet they are still suffering from the same eating disorder.

Websites

http://edauk.com/mens-issues.htm
The Eating Disorders Association's website has a specific section on men's issues.

Activity 62 Revision summary – Eating disorders

Objective

To identify clinical characteristics, explanations and research studies relating to anorexia nervosa and bulimia nervosa.

Introduction

Anorexia nervosa (AN) and bulimia nervosa (BN) are eating disorders characterised by physically and/or psychologically harmful eating patterns. The AS specification requires knowledge on the clinical characteristics, explanations and research studies on AN and BN.

HOW DO YOU DO IT?

Complete the flow diagram on the next page.
Read Gross, McIlveen *et al.* (2000), pages 107–113 to help you fill in the boxes. This will be a particularly useful aid to revision.

Notes

It may be helpful to double the size of the flow diagram, so there is sufficient room to include all the relevant details.

Homework

Describe and evaluate any two explanations for anorexia nervosa (300 words maximum).

Activity 62 **Flow diagram**

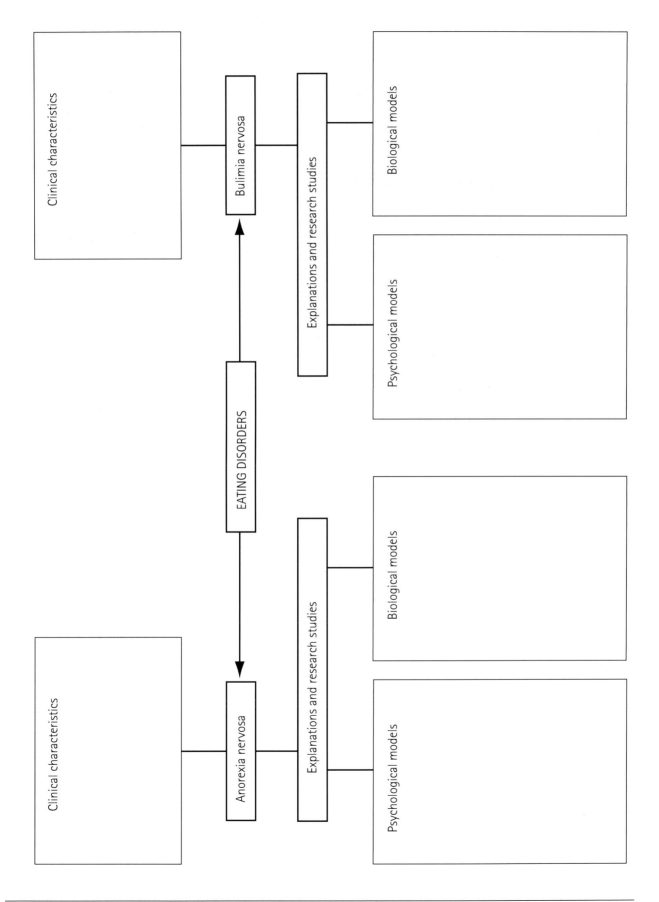

Activity 63 Revision Summary: Individual differences

Defining psychological abnormality

Define and identify at least two limitations of the following definitions of abnormality:
• abnormality as statistical infrequency
• abnormality as deviation from social norms
• abnormality as deviation from ideal mental health
• abnormality as a failure to function adequately.

Biological and psychological models of abnormality

Outline the major causes of abnormal behaviour and the implications for treatment according to the following models of abnormality:
• the biological model
• the psychodynamic model
• the behavioural model
• the cognitive model.

Critical issue: eating disorders

Identify the clinical characteristics of anorexia nervosa and bulimia nervosa.
Explain each disorder in relation to biological and psychological models of abnormality. Make sure that, for each model, you describe at least one research study, including details of the research aims, participants, procedures, conclusions and significance of the chosen study to our understanding of eating disorders.

Activity 64 Multiple choice questions

1 Which definition of abnormality refers to abnormal behaviour as that which 'deviates from the average':
   a deviation from ideal mental health
   b statistical infrequency
   c failure to function adequately
   d maladaptiveness.

2 Identify one problem in defining abnormal behaviour as 'statistical infrequency':
   a it fails to take into account the desirability of a behaviour
   b it relies on value judgements
   c it is subjective
   d it places too much emphasis on an individual's failure to function adequately.

3 According to the 'deviation from ideal mental health' definition:
   a there are characteristics and abilities which people should possess in order to be considered normal
   b there are no behaviours which can be defined as abnormal so all individuals have ideal mental health
   c abnormal behaviour involves behaving in ways of which society disapproves
   d an individual may be defined as abnormal if s/he behaves in ways in which the majority of individuals would behave.

4 The problem with defining abnormality as deviation from social norms is that:
   a the definition is bound by culture
   b it is an imprecise definition, which is prone to subjectivity
   c the definition is too era-dependent
   d a, b and c.

5 The demonological model of abnormality has been replaced by:
   a medical model and psychological models including the psychodynamic, behavioural and cognitive models
   b medicinal model and psychosocial models
   c medicine man's model
   d psychological models, including the psychodynamic, behavioural and cognitive models.

6 Therapies based on the medical model do not include:
   a electroconvulsive therapy
   b chemotherapy
   c cognitive therapy
   d psychosurgery.

7 The psychodynamic approach sees abnormality as based on:
   a faulty learning processes
   b unresolved and unconscious sexual conflicts that originate in childhood
   c faulty thinking processes
   d biochemical imbalances.

8 Which one of the following is not a defence mechanism:
   a repression
   b displacement
   c humour
   d regression.

9 According to the psychodynamic approach, treatment of abnormal behaviour involves:
   a accessing conscious thought processes and suppressing them into the unconscious
   b making unconscious thoughts conscious
   c reducing the client to a state of unconsciousness
   d systematic desensitisation.

10 Which of the following criticisms does not apply to the psychodynamic approach:
   a the sample of participants on which Freud based his theory was not representative
   b the theory cannot be tested scientifically
   c the empirical evidence underlying this theory is based on case study evidence and prone to subjective interpretation
   d the theory does not provide a detailed and comprehensive account of abnormality.

11 The main assumption of the behavioural model is that:
   a abnormal behaviours are the result of faulty thought processes
   b abnormal behaviours are the result of unconscious sexual desires
   c abnormal behaviours are the result of faulty learning, and are acquired in the same way as normal behaviour, through the processes of classical and operant conditioning
   d abnormal behaviours are the result of genetic factors.

12 Who carried out a case study demonstrating the role of classical conditioning in the development of a phobia:
   a Watson and Holmes
   b Wilkins and Rayner
   c Watson and Rayner
   d Ivan Pavlov.

13 In the case of 'Little Albert', Albert acquired a phobia by a process of:
   a operant conditioning
   b classically operant conditioning
   c operant classical conditioning
   d classical conditioning.

14 Which of the following are therapies based on operant conditioning techniques:
   a flooding
   b aversion therapy
   c token economy programmes
   d systematic desensitisation.

15 According to the cognitive approach, mental disorders are caused by:
   a meditational processes
   b mediating processes
   c environmental processes
   d inner conflicts.

16 According to the biological approach, which of the following may explain the origin of anorexia nervosa:
   a genetics
   b changes in levels of neurotransmitters
   c dysfunction of the hypothalamus
   d all of these.

17 Who investigated the concordance rate of anorexia nervosa in monozygotic twins?
   a Cnattingius *et al.*
   b Askevold and Heiberg
   c Bruch
   d Minuchin *et al.*

18 A concordance rate of 50 per cent for monozygotic twins suggests that:
   a genes play an important role in the development of anorexia
   b genes play an important role but other factors (e.g. social/environmental) may also contribute to the development of anorexia nervosa
   c genes do not play an important role in the development of anorexia nervosa
   d social factors play a very important social role.

19 Which of the following may account for the development of bulimia nervosa?
   a cholecystokinin octapeptide
   b plasma endorphins
   c serotonin
   d all of these.

20 Which of the following provides the best explanation accounting for the development of anorexia and bulimia nervosa:
   a the biological approach
   b the psychological approaches, including psychodynamic, behavioural and cognitive
   c the multidimensional risk perspective
   d none of these.

Answers to Activity 64

   1 b
   2 a
   3 a
   4 d
   5 a
   6 c
   7 b
   8 c
   9 b
  10 d
  11 c
  12 c
  13 d
  14 c
  15 b
  16 d
  17 b
  18 b
  19 d
  20 c

5 Social Psychology: Social Influence

Specification topic	Gross, McIlveen et al. (2000) 2nd edition	Activity	Page
Conformity and minority influence	**116–126**		
Research into conformity (Sherif, Asch, Zimbardo)	117–121 133–134	65 Norm formation in an ambiguous situation 66 Is conformity desirable or undesirable?	113 114
Minority influence (Moscovici, Clark)	121–122	67 Minority influence in the real world. 68 *Twelve Angry Men*	115 116
Explanations for conformity and minority influence	122–124	69 Why do we conform?	117
Obedience to authority	**126–135**		
Obedience research studies (Milgram, Hofling, Meeus and Raajimakers)	126–132	70 Does the end justify the means? 71 A naturalistic observation of obedience 72 Hofling *et al.* (1966) Obedience in a hospital setting 73 Revision exercise: obedience to authority 74 Factors affecting obedience rates	118 119 120 121 123
Issues of experimental and ecological validity	133	75 Issues of experimental and ecological validity in studies of obedience	125
Psychological explanations for obeying and resisting	133–134	76 A case study of obedience: Adolf Eichmann 77 Resisting pressures to obey	127 129
Ethical issues in psychological research	**136–142**		
Issues of deception, informed consent and protection of participants and the use of ethical guidelines to overcome such problems	136–142	78 Ethical guidelines and Milgram's (1963) study of obedience	131
The relevance of ethical issues in the context of social influence research	136–142	79 Evaluating the prison simulation experiment, Zimbardo *et al.* (1973)	133
Additional work	–	80 Revision summary sheet 81 Multiple choice questions	134 135

General textbooks

1 **Gross, R. and McIlveen, R**. (1998) *Psychology: A New Introduction.* Hodder & Stoughton.
2 **Gross, R.** (1996) *Psychology: The Science of Mind and Behaviour,* Third edition. Hodder & Stoughton.

Activity 65 Norm formation in an ambiguous situation

Objective

To demonstrate that in an ambiguous situation we look to others to provide information and conform accordingly.

Introduction

This activity is a simple demonstration of conformity and norm formation adapted from an early study in this area by Jenness (1932).

Materials

Jam jar and small sweets to fill it.

HOW DO YOU DO IT?

- Fill a jam jar with small sweets.
- Pass the jar round the group. Each person write down their own guess as to how many sweets there are in the jar. Do not confer.
- Write all the answers on the board. Discuss these estimates. Points to consider include the range of answers, outliers and whether there is a group norm.
- Pass the jar round the group again and each person write down a second guess.
- Write all these answers on the board. Discuss these second estimates and again consider the range of answers, outliers and whether there is a group norm.
- Eat the sweets.
- To discuss: What differences do you notice about the two sets of guesses? Can you explain what has occurred here?

Notes

- Jenness (1932) asked students to estimate the number of beans in a bottle and then arranged for the students to discuss their guesses in groups. When asked again for their estimates, the range of answers was reduced, as their guesses shifted towards a group norm. In a situation such as this, when we are unsure, we look to others to provide information to ensure we have a correct perception of reality (informational influence).
- A variation of this activity can be conducted by dividing the class into two groups. Instead of pooling the estimates on the board, present each group with a prepared set of answers, consisting of either high or low estimates. How does this influence the second estimates? Compare the responses of the two groups.
- An alternative to this activity is to replicate Sherif's (1935) study. You will need to blackout a room completely; black sugar paper covering the windows works best. The autokinetic effect can be achieved using a very small light that does not emit a beam. Three volunteers can give their estimates individually and then come together as a group and give their estimates one at a time. The rest of the class can observe the whole process and one member record the findings.

Homework

Read Gross, McIlveen *et al.* (2000), page 117 and take notes that describe and evaluate Sherif's (1935) study of conformity. Compare the procedure and findings of Sherif's study to the main Activity 66, above. Note that we could argue these are examples of norm formation rather than conformity, as there is no 'majority' to conform to.

Activity 66 Is conformity desirable or undesirable?

Objective

To assess the function of conformity in society.

Introduction

There is an underlying assumption in the way studies of conformity have been interpreted that independence is desirable and dependence undesirable. However, conformity facilitates everyday interactions with others. It makes the world more predictable and the process provides us with valuable information on which to structure our social behaviour. A society could not function without conforming behaviour.

Materials

Newspapers on CD-ROM.

HOW DO YOU DO IT?

- In groups of four identify specific situations when conformity is desirable or undesirable

	Desirable	Undesirable
1		
2		
3		

- Access the newspapers on CD-ROM. Find an article reporting an event when conformity was demonstrated. Suggest reasons for the conformity occurring. Was the conformity desirable or undesirable?
  Take, for example, *The Guardian*, 13 March 2000, 'Tension in Berlin: Anti-Nazis counter pro-Haider march', by Tony Paterson
- Read and take notes from Gross, McIlveen *et al.* (2000), page 124, to consolidate your learning. Note in particular that Zimbardo & Lieppe (1991) consider conformity to be a valuable social tool in that it 'lubricates the machinery of social interaction [and] enables us to structure our social behaviour and predict the reactions of others.'

Notes

Whether or not we consider conformity desirable is influenced by whether we live in an individualist or collectivist culture. Read and take notes from Gross, McIlveen *et al.* (2000), pages 120–121, and Box 6.7. page 124.

Homework

What are the dangers of conformity? (100 words maximum.)

Essential reading

Gross, McIlveen *et al.* (2000), page 124 'Conformity: good or bad?'

Activity 67 Minority influence in the real world

Objective

To analyse the process of minority influence.

Introduction

Not only can a group influence an individual, an individual can influence a group. There are many examples in history of scientists, artists and politicians who have changed the beliefs of the majority and revolutionised society. In this exercise the process of how minorities are able to initiate changes in the majority view is analysed.

Materials

Overhead transparencies and pens for writing on them.

HOW DO YOU DO IT?

- Working in pairs, identify two minority groups who have had an influence on majority opinion (e.g. animal welfare campaigners).
- Go to the library and research how your chosen group managed to become influential. Points to consider include: Who did the group consist of? How did they present their arguments? What action did they take?
- Preview Gross, McIlveen *et al.* (2000), Box 6.4 on page 121, a summary of the factors important in minority influence. How well do the behavioural styles of your chosen minority groups match the factors identified here?
- Prepare an overhead transparency to feedback your findings to the rest of the group.

Notes

- Minorities resist pressures to conform and this type of dissent is an important factor in democratic societies.
- New forms of art, political change and the development of science, have largely depended on minority influence.

Essential reading

Gross, McIlveen *et al.* (2000), page 121 'How do minorities exert an influence?'

Homework

Minorities are often ridiculed before they are taken seriously. List examples of influential minorities who were not initially taken seriously.
Social change is more often the result of minority influence than majority influence. Do any of your examples concern minorities that have changed the course of human history? (200 words maximum.)

 ctivity 68 Twelve Angry Men

Objective

To analyse the process of minority influence in the film *Twelve Angry Men*.

Introduction

In the film *Twelve Angry Men*, Henry Fonda plays the part of one juror, who along with 11 other jurors have to decide over the guilt or innocence of a young man charged with murder. At the outset of the deliberations, all members of the jury panel are convinced of the man's guilt except for Henry Fonda's character. How this lone juror manages to persuade the others of the defendant's innocence is the focus of the film and provides a detailed example of minority influence.

Materials

Film – 'Twelve Angry Men'.

HOW DO YOU DO IT?

Watch the film and then in pairs answer the following questions:

1 How is Henry Fonda's character (the minority) first viewed by the other jurors (the majority)? Note down any illustrative quotes.
2 How is Fonda's character made to feel?
3 How does Fonda's character present his argument persuasively? What techniques does he use?
4 Are there factors about his personality characteristics and/or physical appearance pertinent to his successful persuasion?
5 Can you identify specific examples of both conformity and compliance in the film?
6 Distinguish between the normative influence and informational influence operating in the deliberation process.

Notes

To discuss: Is there any evidence of obedience in the film?

Homework

Draw a flow diagram to summarise the process of minority influence and the sequence of events in the film. Include the results of each ballot, the evidence presented by Fonda's character at each stage and the reactions of the different jurors.

Web reference

http://us.imdb.com/Title?0050083
This film review includes an overview of the character of each juror in the film.

(A)ctivity 69 Why do we conform?

Objective

To analyse the reasons for conforming in everyday life.

Introduction

Conformity is a crucial process in social living. Whether we like the idea of 'conforming' or not, we all conform in everyday life to some extent. This exercise reveals the main motivational factors behind everyday examples of conformity.

HOW DO YOU DO IT?

Working in pairs discuss the main motivation for each of the following conforming behaviours and write down your answers:

- agreeing to see a film at the cinema that interests your friends but not you
- ordering a coffee in a restaurant because your three friends have done so
- laughing at a joke you don't understand because others around do
- dressing in a smart, but uncomfortable, outfit to go to a wedding because you expect the other guests to be dressed in a formal style
- crossing a road at a red light because you see others do so
- joining the end of a queue at a bus stop
- turning on your headlights when driving in the rain because you see other drivers doing so
- agreeing to split a restaurant bill equally, even though you did not have a starter when others did
- at a buffet, only helping yourself to a small amount even though you are hungry
- remaining silent in a class discussion even though you disagree with all that is being said.

Can you think of any other examples of conforming behaviours?

Notes

- The reasons for conforming are varied but usually involve:
  - informational influence; the need to have a correct perception of reality leads us to look to others for information when we are uncertain how to behave
  - normative influence; the need to be approved of and liked leads us to behave as others are in order to be accepted.
- Characteristics of the majority, such as the size of the group, their status and their power, will influence whether an individual will conform.
- Characteristics of the individual, such as their personality and gender, will influence whether they conform.

Homework

Read Gross, McIlveen *et al.* (2000), pages 122–123 and take notes to distinguish between the two major types of conformity, internalisation and compliance. Look again at the list of behaviours above. Which involve internalisation and which involve compliance?

Web reference

http://www.science.wayne.edu/~wpoff/cor/grp/influenc.html
This site focuses on four aspects of social influence: conformity, compliance, obedience and sources of social influence.

Activity 70 Does the end justify the means?

Objective

To examine the moral significance of the Milgram experiments.

Introduction

The study of obedience from a psychological perspective originated from the atrocities of the Second World War. The perpetrators were believed to be different from ordinary people and this explanation was used to interpret the Nazis' behaviour. Milgram's experiments provided an alternative explanation, demonstrating that ordinary people will be obedient to the point of severely harming others.

HOW DO YOU DO IT?

Topic for debate: 'Stanley Milgram carried out some of the most morally significant research in modern psychology.'

- Preview Gross, McIlveen *et al.* (2000), pages 126–132.
- The teacher should act as chairperson. The chairperson's role is to introduce the motion and take a vote, provide an introduction by briefly summarising Milgram's experiment and the commentary that ensued, introduce each speaker, provide a summary and take a closing vote.
- Divide the rest of the group into three teams.
- Team A: Build up a case to support the motion. Elect a speaker.
- Team B: Build a case to challenge the motion. Elect a speaker.
- Team C: Think of questions you would like to ask each side.

Notes

- Note Milgram's quote on page 130 of Gross, McIlveen *et al.* (2000), 'The most fundamental lesson of our study is that ordinary people simply doing their jobs, and without any particular hostility on their part, can become agents in a terrible, destructive process.'
- It is likely that some of the criticisms of Milgram's experiment arise because of the unanticipated findings. It is easier to accept that the experimenter was 'cruel' and that some people are 'evil' rather than the findings that ordinary people are capable of behaving in a callous and inhumane way as a result of social pressure.

Homework

1 Explain what is meant by the term 'obedience' (3 marks).
2 To what extent can Milgram's research on obedience be justified? (12 marks).
(250 words maximum).

Web reference

http://muskingum.edu/~psychology/psychweb/history/milgram.htm
This 'Milgram' site includes biography, time line, bibliography and an overview of his theory.

Activity 71 A naturalistic observation of obedience

Objective

To investigate obedience to the law in a naturalistic setting.

Introduction

In many cases psychologists simply observe the behaviour of people in a given situation, sacrificing rigid control over variables in favour of ecological validity. Naturalistic observation is probably the only ethically sound method of studying obedience and the law provides an accessible situation.

Materials

Overhead transparencies and appropriate pens.

HOW DO YOU DO IT?

- In groups of three, choose the behaviour you will observe. Ideas include: whether drivers stop at zebra crossings, whether drivers wear seatbelts.
- Agree your procedure. Points to consider include length of observation and number of participants.
- Construct a table to record your results and conduct your study.
- Discuss whether you can explain your findings.
- Make brief notes on the aim, method and results of this study.
- Prepare an overhead transparency to feedback your findings to the rest of the group.

Notes

- Agree with the teacher where you will observe the behaviour you choose. It must be a safe place.
- Variations of this activity include recording gender differences in the behaviour you choose. Read Gross, McIlveen *et al.* (2000), page 129. Did Milgram (1963) find gender differences when the participants were women?

Homework

Evaluate your study in as much detail as possible. Points to consider include: consistency between different observers and observer bias, ethical issues and the advantages/disadvantages of the observational method. Read Gross, McIlveen *et al.* (2000), pages 148–150 for help with these issues (200 words maximum).

Activity 72 Hofling et al. (1966): obedience in a hospital setting

Objective

To describe and evaluate Hofling *et al.*'s (1966) naturalistic study of obedience in a hospital setting.

Introduction

Milgram's experiments have been criticised for their lack of ecological validity (mundane realism). However, his findings are supported by a study conducted by Hofling *et al.* (1966). This was a naturalistic study of nurses in a hospital setting that also found high levels of obedience. In this exercise the Hofling study is described and evaluated including a consideration of ethical issues.

HOW DO YOU DO IT?

- Read Gross, McIlveen *et al.* (2000), pages 131–132, Box 6.11, Hofling *et al.*'s (1966) naturalistic study of nurses.
- Working in groups of three, discuss the following questions:
  - For what practical reasons might disobedience have been difficult for the nurses?
  - Why is it important to note that the study was conducted in 1966?
  - What are the implications of Hofling *et al.*'s study?
  - Compare the findings from the control group, presented with the situation as a scenario, to the results of Milgram's pre-experiment prediction survey (see Gross, McIlveen *et al.* 2000, page 128). How can these findings be explained?
  - Was the study ethical? Consider issues of informed consent, deception, protection of participants and withdrawal from the investigation.

Notes

A variation of this activity is for each group to record their discussion points on an overhead transparency and for two groups to be chosen at random to present their findings to the class.

Homework

Summarise your discussion points (200 words maximum).

Activity 73 Revision exercise: obedience to authority

Objective

To describe and evaluate research studies of obedience.

Introduction

This activity tests knowledge of research studies of obedience and reveals areas for further revision.

HOW DO YOU DO IT?

- Working in pairs, fill in as much of the diagram (on the next page) as you can, from memory.
- In a different coloured pen, use your class notes and textbook to complete the rest of the diagram.
- Consolidate your knowledge of the concepts you could not remember.

Notes

- A variation of this activity could be for half the group to use the diagram provided and half the group to construct their own revision diagram. It is useful to compare the completed work and discuss the benefits of the different revision techniques.
- Construct a similar revision diagram for research studies of conformity. Headings could include:
  - Sherif (1935)
  - Asch (1953)
  - Zimbardo *et al.* (1973)
  - Moscovici *et al.* (1969)
  - a comparison of the processes of majority and minority influence
  - definitions of key terms.

Activity 73 Revision diagram

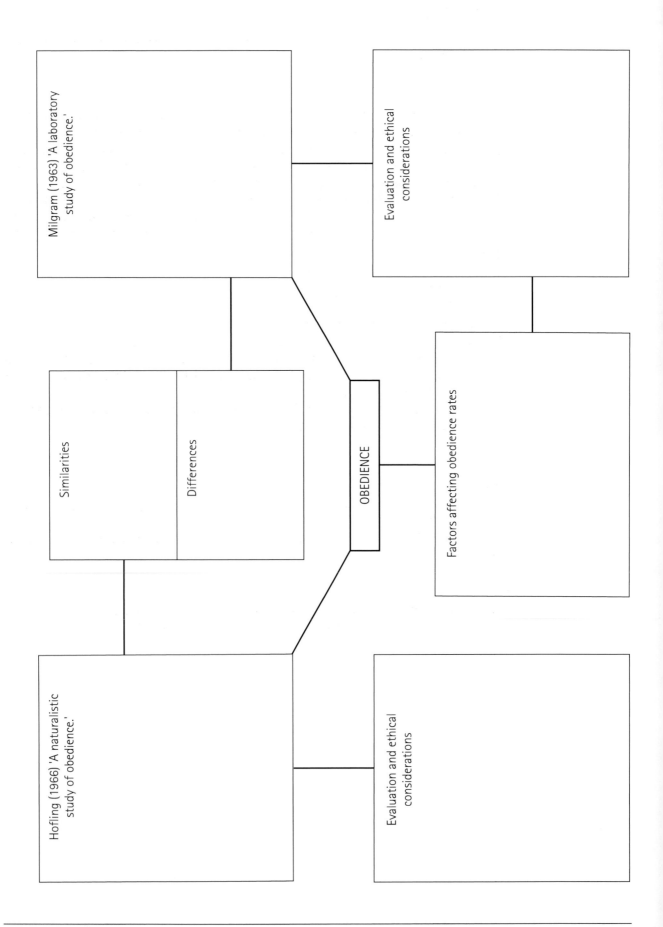

Milgram (1963) 'A laboratory study of obedience.'

Evaluation and ethical considerations

Similarities

Differences

OBEDIENCE

Factors affecting obedience rates

Hofling (1966) 'A naturalistic study of obedience.'

Evaluation and ethical considerations

Activity 74 Factors affecting obedience rates

Objective

To describe the procedural variations of Milgram's study and the effects of these on obedience rates.

Introduction

In his original study Milgram (1963) found a 65 per cent obedience rate. His results were entirely unexpected, partly because in a pre-experiment survey at Yale University, Milgram had presented the procedure as a scenario to staff and students and had asked them to estimate the percentage of participants that would obey. The staff mean estimate was 0.1 per cent and the student mean estimate 1.2 per cent. Milgram decided after the initial experiment to investigate what it was about the situation that caused participants to obey. He conducted a series of 18 experiments, each time altering one aspect of the original procedure. In this Activity seven of these variations are considered.

HOW DO YOU DO IT?

- Working in pairs, complete the table on the next page.
- In the first column the procedural variations of Milgram's study are described. Working in pairs, discuss how you think the procedural variation may have affected the obedience rate (try to give an estimated percentage) and write down your answer in the second column. Give the reason for your answer.
- Now read Gross, McIlveen *et al.* (2000), pages 129–130 and complete the third column of the table with Milgram's actual findings.

Notes

- 'Obedience rate' is taken as the percentage of participants that administered the maximum 450-volt shock.
- What do these findings tell us about independent behaviour? Remember that in some situations many participants did not obey.

Homework

Identify and describe six features common to the original procedure and the variations that can help explain why some participants obeyed (200 words maximum).

Activity 74 **Response sheet**

Variations of Milgram's original procedure

Procedural variation	Estimated obedience rate	Actual obedience rate
Institutional context: the experiment took place in a run-down office building.		
Proximity: the teacher and learner were in the same room (about 46 cm apart).		
Touch proximity: the teacher was required to force the learner's hand down onto the shock plate.		
Remote authority: the experimenter gave initial instructions to the teacher in person and then left the room and gave all further instructions by telephone.		
Two peers rebel: the teacher was only required to deliver the shocks and two other teachers (confederates) read the word pairs and informed the learner if the response was correct; at 150 volts one confederate teacher refused to continue and at 210 volts the second confederate teacher followed.		
A peer administers the shock: the teacher was required only to read out the word pairs and another teacher (a confederate) delivered the shocks.		
Female participants: the original procedure was followed with female teachers.		

Activity 75 Issues of experimental and ecological validity in studies of obedience

Objective

To discuss issues of experimental and ecological validity in studies of obedience.

Introduction

If you had been a participant in Milgram's study, how would you have reacted to the highly unusual situation you found yourself in? For the vast majority of people, being asked to deliberately cause harm to another person would be outside the range of their experience. Would you really believe that you were administering electric shocks? Would you react differently in a real-life situation? These questions have been debated since the Milgram experiments were conducted and by addressing them we can assess how much these findings tell us about the process of obedience in real-life situations.

HOW DO YOU DO IT?

Working in pairs, complete the worksheet on the next page. Fill in the blanks and discuss your responses to each question before writing your answer.

Notes

- Although Hofling *et al.*'s (1966) study is usually considered to be high in ecological validity this has been disputed. Can you identify aspects of the study that make it artificial?
- To discuss: Comment on the experimental and ecological validity of Zimbardo *et al.*'s (1972) prison simulation experiment. Compare this to Milgram's study.

Homework

'The process of obedience, as observed in studies, is a reflection of the processes of obedience in real-life situations.' Discuss (200 words maximum).

Activity *75* **Response sheet**

Issues of experimental and ecological validity in studies of obedience

If an experiment has an impact on the participants, forces them to take it seriously and involves them in the procedures then it is said to have

_____.

The similarity of the laboratory experiment to the events which commonly happen to people in the real world is referred to as _____.

Experimental validity

Orne & Holland (1968) have criticised Milgram's study and suggest that the participants did not really believe the experimental set-up and knew the learner was not really being given electric shocks (i.e. they were merely role-playing in the experiment).

They also proposed that obedience in the Milgram experiments is a result of demand characteristics – the cues in the environment that influence the participants' perceptions of what is required of them. Obeying the experimenter is a demand characteristic of any experiment.

Evidence

1 Does the participants' behaviour during Milgram's experiment suggest that they believed the experimental set-up?
2 Some participants did not obey and administer the full 450 volts. What does this suggest about the experimental validity of the experiment?
3 Write down a summary of Sheridan & King's (1972) study from Gross, McIlveen *et al.* (2000), page 131, Box 6.10. Do the findings support Milgram's claim that his study has experimental validity?

Ecological validity

Orne & Holland (1968) have argued that the results of Milgram's study only inform us about obedience in an artificial laboratory setting. They challenge the generalizability of the findings and propose that the situation in Milgram's study is very different from real-life situations that require obedience. However, Milgram argues that that the essential process involved in complying with the demands of an authority figure is the same, whether the setting is contrived in a laboratory, or naturally occurring in the real world.

Evidence

1 Comment on the ecological validity of Hofling *et al.*'s study (Gross, McIlveen *et al.* 2000, pages 131–132, Box 6.11). Do the findings support or contradict Milgram's claims?
2 Is there cross-cultural support for the ecological validity of Milgram's study? (Refer to Gross, McIlveen *et al.* 2000, page 132, Table 6.3.)

Activity 76 A case study of obedience: Adolf Eichmann

Objective

To apply psychological explanations for obeying to the case of Adolf Eichmann.

Introduction

Milgram's (1963) studies have been criticised for lacking mundane realism, that is, for bearing little relevance to obedience in the real world. In this exercise some of the factors identified in the Milgram studies as increasing the likelihood of obedience are applied to an infamous case study of obedience.

HOW DO YOU DO IT?

- Read and make notes on the three social processes involved in genocide, Box 6.12 in Gross, McIlveen *et al.* (2000), page 133.
- Read the summary below of the psychological explanations for obeying.

Diffusion of responsibility the tendency for individuals to feel less personal responsibility for their actions when they are obeying instructions. The responsibility is perceived to be that of the authority figure. Milgram called this 'operating in the agentic state' i.e. as an agent of others, when our individual conscience ceases to influence our actions.

Buffers are any aspect of a situation that shields the individual from having to face the consequences of their actions, thus making the obedience easier.

Gradual commitment is the process by which an individual may readily obey when only a little is asked for but this ensures a feeling of commitment when demands are increased. If the demands are graduated it becomes more difficult to disobey at any point as the demands only vary in a small way from previous demands that were obeyed.

- In groups of four, discuss to what extent the processes outlined above help to explain the following case study.
- Individually write a summary of your discussion points (150 words).

Arendt (1963) reported the trial of the Nazi war criminal Adolf Eichmann – one of the people responsible for the concentration camp programme. She reported what an ordinary man he seemed to be, rather than the 'monster' most people imagined. Despite him being responsible for the death of six million Jews, Eichmann had originally argued for a separate homeland for the Jews, and had personally helped his cousin, who was half Jewish, to escape. His self-perception was one of a dutiful officer – one aspect of which was obeying orders. Despite his central role of responsibility, Eichmann had negligible contact with the concentration camps and the officers on the ground. When he did see for himself the 'death trains' he had been organising, he was physically sick, but he did not change his work.

Notes

- Make a list of other infamous examples of blind obedience.
- Milgram's studies and real life events show that we need to be educated about the dangers of blind obedience.

Homework

Are we ever able to justify abdicating responsibility for our actions with the claim 'I was only following orders'?

On what basis do we place people in positions of responsibility in our society? (200 words maximum.)

Web reference

http://www.sonoma.edu/people/g/goodman/zimbardo.htm

This is the text of the lecture 'Transforming people into Perpetrators of Evil' that Zimbardo gave to the Holocaust Studies Centre, Sonoma State University in March 1999. It includes applications of the research in this area to several real-life events.

A*ctivity* 77 Resisting pressures to obey

Objective

To apply strategies for reducing blind obedience.

Introduction

Some of the participants in the Milgram experiment and in other studies of obedience resisted the commands to obey and behaved independently. As well as addressing the question 'Why do we obey?' it is just as important to ask 'Why do we disobey?' Milgram's findings revealed that ordinary people are capable of acting in an inhumane way as a result of social pressure, so ordinary people should become aware of the dangers of blind obedience. In this exercise raising awareness in a practical way is explored.

Materials

Overhead transparencies, appropriate pens and an overhead projector.

HOW DO YOU DO IT?

Milgram himself concluded that there were several ways in which obedience could be reduced:

Educating people about the dangers of blind obedience

Evidence: Gamson *et al.* (1982) invited citizens of a small American town to a hotel conference in order to discuss community standards. The researchers explained that a local petrol station manager had publicly opposed high petrol prices and that the petrol company was taking legal action against him. The participants were asked to speak out against the petrol station manager and to allow their videotaped discussions to be used in court (i.e. they were asked to falsify evidence).

Encouraging them to question authority

Evidence: Hofling *et al.* (1966) observed nurses when told, by a confederate posing as a doctor on the telephone, to administer a drug without written authorisation at a dosage above the daily maximum. Twenty-one out of the 22 nurses obeyed. The nurses were working in an environment that required unquestioning obedience to a superior, in this case a doctor.

Exposing them to the actions of disobedient models

Evidence: in a variation of Milgram's original study the teacher was paired with two other (stooge) teachers. The stooges refused to continue, one at 150 volts and the other at 250 volts. There was a 10 per cent obedience rate. In a situation beyond the range of their experience the participants looked to others for information and observed that it was possible to disobey.

- In groups of four, plan a one hour tutorial lesson, suitable for a 12–14 age group, to explore the dangers of blind obedience. In your lesson you might like to include research evidence, role-play, group activities, discussion, etc.
- Prepare an overhead transparency/flipchart to feedback your lesson plan to the rest of the class.

Notes

- Another reason for resisting the demands of an authority figure may be an individual's past experiences. One particular participant in Milgram's research not only refused to obey but showed few signs of anxiety or stress during the procedure. During post-experimental interviews it was revealed that Gretchan Brandt had grown up in Nazi Germany. She claimed to have seen too much pain in her life for her to continue with the experiment.
- Reactance is a process of resisting the demands of an authority figure, this is when an individual responds with a behaviour or attitude that is the opposite of what is being requested. This can occur when an individual feels their sense of freedom is being threatened. The increase in smoking among young people may well be the result of reactance. Can you think of other examples of reactance?
- Make a list of practical ways to resist conformity and peer pressure.

Homework

Under what circumstances are we less likely to obey an authority figure? (100 words maximum.)

Activity 78 Ethical guidelines and Milgram's (1963) study of obedience

Objective

To understand ethical guidelines and apply them to Milgram's (1963) study.

Introduction

Ethical issues in psychology are an area of study in their own right. Originally it was expected that psychologists would incorporate ethical concerns into their experimental design and that decisions regarding ethical issues would be taken by the individual experimenter. As a result of controversies such as those surrounding Milgram's work ethical guidelines underlie all psychological research today. The British Psychological Society (BPS) produces ethical guidelines which are intended to protect the rights and dignity of all those who participate in research in this country. In this exercise ethical issues are examined and applied to Milgram's (1963) study of obedience.

HOW DO YOU DO IT?

- Working in groups of four, imagine you are on a panel of people who give permission for psychological research to go ahead. Make a list of guidelines that you think should be in place to prevent unethical research taking place.
- Preview Gross, McIlveen *et al.* (2000), pages 136–142, a summary of the existing British Psychological Society ethical guidelines. Did you think about all these issues? Did you think of anything else?
- Complete the table on the next page 'An ethical evaluation of Milgram's study'.
- Compare your completed table to another group's. Did you present similar arguments?

Homework

Ethical guidelines are periodically reviewed and updated. Read Gross, McIlveen *et al.* (2000), page 139 and take notes on why and how this process occurs.

Web reference

http://www.bps.org.uk/charter/codofcon.htm
This website includes the code of conduct for chartered psychologists and supplements the ethical guidelines published by the BPS.

Further reading

'Obeying Orders', from the *Sunday Telegraph Magazine*, October 8 2000, pages 19–27.
This detailed account of Milgram's work includes an interview with Herbert Winer, one of the participants in the original study.

Activity 78 Response sheet

An ethical evaluation of Milgram's study

The study was not ethical	Milgram's defence

Activity 79 Evaluating the prison simulation experiment (Zimbardo et al., 1973)

Objective

To evaluate the prison simulation experiment in terms of ethical issues.

Introduction

Social norms and roles provide us with guidelines in terms of how we should behave and how we expect others to behave. They are therefore valuable in the functioning of society. The aim of the prison simulation experiment was to simulate the psychological effects of imprisonment through role-playing. However, the findings demonstrated dramatically the dangers of conforming to social roles and the power attributed to prescribed positions within society. In this activity the ethical issues underlying the experiment are explored.

HOW DO YOU DO IT?

- Access the following website: http://www.prisonexp.org/.
  This website provides a detailed account of the prison simulation experiment and includes archival photographs of each stage of the experiment.
- Working in groups of four, discuss the ethical issues arising from this experiment. Take notes to summarise your discussion points.
- Access the following website: http://www.stanford.edu/dept/news/relaged/970108prison-exp.html.
  This website provides an account of the experiment from the perspective of Christina Maslach, who observed parts of the original study and is credited for being the person responsible for its early termination.
- The website reports that Zimbardo himself has mixed feeling about the ethics of his experiment. Take notes to summarise the reasons why he considers it ethical and the reasons why he considers it unethical.

Notes

In the second website re-read the section 'Lives redirected'. The experiment has had long-term effects on the lives of both the participants and experimenters. Have these effects been negative or positive? Review the summary of the ethical guidelines currently published by the British Psychological Society. Do they account for the possibility of such long-term effects?

Homework

The account of Maslach's versions of events includes evidence of several aspects of social influence both in the prison and amongst the experimenters. Can you identify the processes of minority influence, obedience, conformity and compliance in this account? (200 words maximum.)

Essential reading

Gross, McIlveen *et al.* (2000), pages 133–135, 'Zimbardo's research'.

Activity *80* Revision summary sheet

- Define the following terms:
  social influence
  conformity
  minority influence
  obedience
  experimental validity
  ecological validity
  compliance

- Describe the aim, method, results, conclusions and two criticisms of one study
  into each of the following:
  conformity
  minority influence
  obedience

- Describe and evaluate one explanation of each of the following:
  conformity
  minority influence
  obeying
  resisting

- What is meant by the term 'ethical issues'?

- What are ethical guidelines?

- Explain what is meant by:
  deception
  informed consent
  protection of participants.

- Give two ethical criticisms of one study of social influence.

Activity *81* Multiple choice questions

1 The definition of conformity is:
  a performing a con trick
  b complying with the explicit demands of the group
  c yielding to group pressure, real or imagined
  d yielding to stereotyped expectations.

2 Sherif's (1935) study produced:
  a independent behaviour
  b an ambiguous result
  c a group norm
  d obedience.

3 Asch's (1951) experiment used:
  a critical trials when stooges gave the wrong answers
  b neutral trials when stooges gave the right answers
  c critical trials when stooges gave the right answers
  d both a and b.

4 In Asch's experiment, the number of participants conforming at least once was:
  a 25 per cent
  b 50 per cent
  c 75 per cent
  d 100 per cent.

5 Compliance is:
  a when our public statements are not consistent with our private views
  b a result of informational influence
  c when our public statements are consistent with our private views
  d a result of minority influence.

6 Normative social influence is:
  a the need for acceptance/approval of others
  b the need for certainty
  c influencing others to be independent
  d disagreeing with majority opinion.

7 The original purpose of Milgram's experiment was to test:
  a the 'Germans are a conforming nation' hypothesis
  b the 'Germans are an independent nation' hypothesis
  c the 'Germans are different' hypothesis
  d the 'Germans are just like the Americans' hypothesis.

8 In Milgram's original experiment:
  a 100 per cent of participants administered a 450 volt shock
  b 65 per cent of participants administered a 450 volt shock
  c 55 per cent of participants administered a 450 volt shock
  d 32 per cent of participants administered a 450 volt shock.

9 In a variation of Milgram's experiment in which the teacher was required to force the learner's hand onto the shock plate:
   a none of the participants obeyed
   b 65 per cent of participants administered a 450 volt shock
   c 30 per cent of participants administered a 450 volt shock
   d 5 per cent of participants administered a 450 volt shock.

10 According to Orne & Holland (1968), Milgram's experiment lacked:
   a debriefing
   b experimental realism because the experimental set-up was too realistic
   c experimental realism because the participants did not believe the set-up
   d adequate safety measures.

11 Sheridan & King's (1972) study of obedience using puppies:
   a confirms the experimental validity of Milgram's study
   b had higher ecological validity than Milgram's experiment
   c resulted in obedience levels of 30 per cent
   d resulted in obedience levels of 100 per cent.

12 Which of the following was NOT identified by Milgram as a method of reducing blind obedience:
   a education
   b encouragement to question authority
   c punishing unquestioning obedience
   d exposure to disobedient models.

13 Hofling *et al.*'s (1966) study of obedience in nurses involved:
   a greater mundane realism than Milgram's experiment
   b less mundane realism than Milgram's experiment
   c a biased sample
   d informed consent.

14 Zimbardo *et al.*'s (1973) prison simulation experiment demonstrated:
   a the power of the social situation on individuals' behaviour
   b how role-play turned into a power trip for the guards
   c how role-play turned into real demoralisation for the prisoners
   d all of the above.

15 Zimbardo *et al.*'s (1973) prison simulation experiment was:
   a due to last for two weeks but terminated after 24 hours
   b due to last for two weeks but terminated after six days
   c due to last for two weeks but continued for three weeks
   d none of the above.

16 Milgram concluded that people obey due to:
   a a diffusion of responsibility
   b normative influence
   c fear of ridicule
   d all of the above.

17 Which of the following is NOT a criterion for the protection of participants in experimental studies? The experimenter must:
   a protect participants from physical and mental harm
   b ensure the overall risk of harm is no greater than in normal life
   c protect participants from stress
   d not ask participants about personal or private experiences.

18 Ethical guidelines are updated:
   a in light of the changing social and political contexts in which psychological research takes place
   b to include new ethical problems highlighted by research
   c to include changing views about the nature of individual rights
   d all of the above.

19 Debriefing should:
   a include an apology, in advance, of any adverse publicity
   b allow the participants to leave the experimental situation in the same frame of mind as they entered it
   c allow participants to compare responses
   d include appropriate payment to the participant.

20 Milgram:
   a had his research investigated after publication in 1963
   b had his APA membership suspended in 1963
   c was awarded a prize for outstanding contribution to social psychological research
   d all of the above.

Activity 81 – Answers

   1 c
   2 c
   3 d
   4 c
   5 a
   6 a
   7 c
   8 b
   9 c
   10 c
   11 a
   12 c
   13 a
   14 d
   15 b
   16 a
   17 d
   18 d
   19 b
   20 d

6 Research Methods: Quantitative and Qualitative Methods

Specification topic	Gross, McIlveen et al. (2000) 2nd edition	Activity	Page
• Laboratory experiments	145	82 Quantitative and qualitative research methods	139
• Field experiments	145	83 Summary/evaluation of key research studies	143
• Natural experiments	145	84 Choice of research methods	144
• Correlational analysis	147–148		
• Naturalistic observations	148–150		
• Questionnaire surveys	150–151		
• Interviews	151–152		
Research design and implementation	**155–160**		
• Aims and hypotheses (experimental/alternative /null: one/two tailed)	155	85 Understanding aims and formulating hypotheses	146
• Selection of participants	159–160	86 The selection of participants	148
• Experimental designs (independent, repeated and matched pairs) and naturalistic observation, questionnaire surveys and interview designs	156–158	87 Observing others 88 Designing a questionnaire/survey 89 Conducting interviews	149 150 151
• Use of IV/DV, pilot studies, ways to assess and improve reliability and validity (internal, external and ecological); ethics	155–160	90 Identifying the IV/DV and confounding variables 91 Ethics in psychological research 92 The BPS guidelines and general ethical principles	153 154 156
Data analysis	**164–172**		
• Analysis of qualitative data from observations, questionnaires and interviews	170–172	93 Analysing qualitative data	158
• Measures of central tendency and dispersion (median, mean, mode, range and standard deviation)	164–166	94 Measures of central tendency and dispersion: a quick test 95 Levels of measurement	160 161
• Positive and negative correlations	168–170	96 Which graph?	162
• Use of histograms, bar charts, frequency polygons and scattergraphs	166–170	97 Designing and carrying out an investigation	166
• Additional work	–	98 Revision summary sheet 99 Multiple choice test	168 169

Reading

1 **Gross, R. and McIlveen, R.** (1998) *Psychology: A New Introduction*, Hodder & Stoughton.
2 **Gross, R., McIlveen, R.** *et al.* (2000) *Psychology: A New Introduction*, 2nd edition, Hodder & Stoughton.
3 **Gross, R.** (1996) *Psychology: The Science of Mind and Behaviour*, 3rd edition, Hodder & Stoughton.
4 **Coolican, H.** (1994) *Research Methods and Statistics in Psychology*, Hodder & Stoughton.

Activity 82 Quantitative and qualitative research methods

Objective

To understand the nature and use of different research methods; their advantages and disadvantages.

Introduction

Psychologists have at their disposal many different research methods ranging from the more objective, scientific methods to other, more subjective methods. Each approach has strengths and weaknesses dependent on the nature of the research that one wishes to investigate.

Materials

A3 paper.

HOW DO YOU DO IT?

Get into groups of two or three and research ONE of the following research methods. You will be expected to produce a poster on A3 paper which should include a definition of the research method, three advantages and disadvantages of this method and a description of a classic research study which used this methodology. Try to specifically mention any ethical issues that are associated with the method chosen.
The specified research methods are:

- laboratory experiment
- field experiment
- natural experiment
- correlational analysis
- naturalistic observations
- questionnaire surveys
- interviews
- case studies.

The best posters may be put up around the classroom.

- Each group must present their poster to the rest of the class.
- Distinguish between quantitative and qualitative data (see Gross, McIlveen *et al.* 2000, page 144).
- For each of the research methods above state whether they lend themselves more to quantitative, qualitative data or both, and give reasons for your answers.

Notes

You can always evaluate psychological studies based on methodological criticisms and as such the material covered in this activity is *vital* for the rest of the topics in the specification.

Homework

- Produce a summary table listing three advantages and disadvantages for each of the research methods covered above. There may be a test on these next lesson!
- 'Quasi-experiments' are studies where the researchers lack complete control of all relevant variables. Such things would include 'non-random allocation of participants to groups'. Read page 146 Gross, McIlveen *et al.* (2000) and explain what this means.

Essential reading

- Gross, McIlveen, *et al.* (2000), pages 145–152.
- Coolican, H (1994) *Research Methods and Statistics in Psychology*, Hodder & Stoughton.

Activity 83 Summary/evaluation of key research studies

Objective

To develop summarising and evaluative skills when reading studies in psychology.

Introduction

One of the essential skills that you need to develop in psychology is the ability to skim-read studies, summarise the most important points and evaluate the study in question.

Materials

One A4 summary sheet and one evaluation sheet per group (see following pages).

HOW DO YOU DO IT?

Working in small groups, for each of the studies cited as the research method examples given in Activity 83, fill in a summary sheet and evaluation sheet for the particular research study. A blank summary sheet and evaluation sheet are provided on the following pages.

Notes

- All of the summary and evaluation sheets for each research study could be photocopied into a class booklet for student use.
- This activity can be used throughout all the AS Specification topics, for every key research study. The summary sheets are extremely useful for revision.

Essential reading

Gross, McIlveen *et al.* (2000): page numbers cannot be cited since it is impossible to know which studies have been selected as examples to illustrate the research methods in Activity 83.

Activity 83 Summary sheet

Summary sheet of key research studies

Title:
Author(s):
Key words:
Aim:
Sample:
Method:
Results:
Conclusions:
Issues/implications:

Activity 83 **Evaluation sheet**

Evaluation sheet of key research studies

Title:
Author:
Evaluation points: theory/concepts:
Evaluation points: sample:
Evaluation points: method:
Evaluation points: results:
Evaluation points: conclusions:
Evaluation points: ethics:
Evaluation points: implications/applications:
Any other comments:

Activity 84 Choice of research methods

Objective

To consider methodological design issues associated with different research methods.

Introduction

There are many different research methods used in psychology. Each of them has different strengths and weaknesses and no single method is perfect or better than another. In reality, the most appropriate method is determined by numerous factors, such as the nature and aim of the research and also practical considerations determined by the researcher.

Materials

Overhead transparencies and an overhead projector.

HOW DO YOU DO IT?

Working in groups, each group should think of a research question which they would like to investigate. Some ideas are listed below (it would be preferable if you thought of your own):

- Does violence on television affect children's behaviour?
- Is eyewitness testimony accurate?
- Do day care nurseries have an effect on children's development?
- Are children who attend pre-school classes at an advantage over those children who don't?
- Does neighbourhood overcrowding affect stress levels?
- Can a good memory be developed through practice?
- Are girls more sociable than boys whilst boys are more competitive than girls?
- Is there a positive correlation between temperature and aggression?
- Does noise affect your ability to do homework?
- Is anorexia nervosa caused by family interactions?

Each group should consider how they would study their chosen topic. Address the following points in your discussion:

- How could you measure the concepts (variables) in the research?
- What would be an appropriate sample?
- How would you get hold of your sample?
- What problems can you foresee obtaining your sample?
- What materials/apparatus would you need?
- Which research method would you use?
- What problems can you foresee with this method?
- Are there any potential ethical problems with your research?
- What data would you collect?
- What would you do with this data?

Write down your ideas on an overhead transparency and present your findings to the rest of the class. The other groups should point out ways the study might be improved.

Notes

It is preferable that students choose an area to research which is covered in the AS/A2 Specification. However, this is not essential since it is the research design *process* which is of interest, not the research topic itself.

Homework

Consider why there are so many problems carrying out research on human participants (maximum 150 words).

Essential reading

Gross, McIlveen *et al.* (2000), pages 145–160.

Website reference

http://trochim.human.cornell.edu/tutorial/belue/belue.htm
Fairly advanced, interactive site which goes through how to choose an experimental design.

Activity 85 Understanding aims and formulating hypotheses

Objective

To understand the difference between an aim and a hypothesis and identify the different types of hypotheses.

Introduction

When designing any psychological study, the researcher has to have an aim and a hypothesis. An aim is more general than a hypothesis and tells us *why* the study is being conducted whereas a hypothesis tells us *what* the study is designed to test. Sometimes a hypothesis predicts the direction in which the results are expected to go, e.g. 'An audience presence improves performance.' A hypothesis which predicts the direction of the results is called a 'one-tailed hypothesis' or 'directional' hypothesis.

If a hypothesis does not state the direction, but says that one factor will affect another, or that there will be a difference but doesn't say what that difference will be, then it is called a 'two-tailed hypothesis' or 'non-directional' hypothesis. An example would be, 'An audience presence affects performance.'

HOW DO YOU DO IT?

Consider the following hypothetical research examples:

- A teacher wants to know if psychology students learn better in small classes.
- An insurance company wishes to find out whether young, male drivers drive more safely when carrying passengers in the car.
- A researcher decides to investigate whether babies prefer to look at a real face or a 'scrambled' picture of a face.
- There is a difference in the way that fathers and mothers play with their children.
- Alcohol affects reaction times.
- Boys are greater risk takers than girls.

For each of the above examples, write out an appropriate directional or non-directional experimental (or alternative) and null hypothesis. Decide for yourself whether you think a directional or non-directional hypothesis would be most appropriate.
Try to also identify the independent and dependent variable for each of the above hypotheses.

Notes

The research examples given above are deliberately not referred to as hypotheses. This is because the statements are not formulated precisely enough to count as hypotheses. For this, the variables mentioned should be more precisely operationalised. Students could consider how the variables might be more precisely operationalised in each of the examples given above.

Homework

- Devise a further two directional and two non-directional hypotheses on any psychological topics.
- Look up the website listed below and make a list of five reasons why we might reject the null hypothesis in a psychology experiment. Try the Einstein Cow activity!

Essential reading

Read Gross, McIlveen *et al.* (2000), page 155: 'Supporting hypotheses with significant differences' to consolidate your learning.

Website reference

http://www.stat.purdue.edu/~wescott/Stat301t/Lecture/lect2/hypothesis.html
Details on hypothesis formulation and testing.

Activity 86 The selection of participants

Objective

To understand the procedure for the selection of participants including the use of random sampling.

Introduction

In any investigation, the target population is *every member* of the group to whom our hypothesis may apply. As it is normally impossible to study *all* people undertaking the behaviour, opinion or attitude we wish to study, we have to try to choose a sample that will be representative (typical) of this larger population. A biased sample is one that is not typical of the whole population.

The size of a sample depends upon a number of factors, such as how representative the sample needs to be, the variability within a target population and constraints of time and money. A general rule is that a sample should be sufficiently large to be representative of the larger group but not so large that the study becomes too expensive or time consuming.

HOW DO YOU DO IT?

Define the following sampling types and then list one advantage and one disadvantage associated with each of them:

- random sampling
- stratified sampling
- systematic sampling
- haphazard sampling
- opportunity or convenience sampling.

Let us say you want to investigate people's views of foxhunting in Britain. Outline the sampling method you would choose for collecting the data, where you would conduct the research and the sample size you require. Justify your choice in each case.

Homework

'Size is not everything': explain this comment in terms of psychological research method sampling (150 words maximum).

Essential reading

Read Gross, McIlveen *et al.* (2000), pages 160–161 to consolidate your learning.

Website reference

http://trochim.human.cornell.edu/tutorial/mugo/tutorial.htm
A very detailed site containing information on what a sample is, the purpose of sampling, bias and errors in sampling, selecting a sample, different sample types and sample size.

Activity 87 Observing others

Objective

To demonstrate the methodological problems that observational studies can have and how these can be resolved.

Introduction

Naturalistic observation is unobtrusive observation conducted in a natural setting. It sounds simple in theory, but in practice can be difficult to do in an unbiased, reliable and valid fashion. This activity should highlight some of these difficulties and show how they may be overcome.

HOW DO YOU DO IT?

In small groups, carry out one of the following observational studies to see if:

- more males than females talk in the library.
- whether people sitting in larger social groups look up (scan) less than people in smaller groups.

Before you start, you need to make some sort of tally chart to help you record your observations. Consider how you plan to define and measure the observed behaviours in your studies. You should observe on your own and collate the data afterwards in your group. After the observation discuss any problems you encountered.

Don't make it obvious that you are observing people, since it is likely to make the data invalid, but it is also unethical to embarrass people.

Write answers to the following questions ready for a full class discussion:

1 Were you reliable observers?
2 Suggest how reliability could be tested and improved?
3 Were your observations valid or biased?
4 Suggest ways to check validity in your study.
5 What have you learned from your observations?
6 How could you improve your study?

Notes

There is often confusion over the use of the observational *technique* and use of the observational *method*. The observational technique can be used in a variety of research methods (e.g. Bandura's (1961) BoBo doll study was an experimental method using an observational technique). With the observation method there is no attempt to manipulate the independent variable (e.g. Schaffer & Emerson's (1964) study of attachment).

Homework

Write up your observational study. Summarise the design considerations, method, results (include an appropriate graph) and consider any conclusions that can be drawn (300 words maximum).

Essential reading

Read Gross, McIlveen *et al.* (2000), pages 159–160 to consolidate your knowledge.

Website reference

http://trochim.human.cornell.edu/tutorial/brown/LauraTP.htm
This web page is designed as an introduction to the basic issues and design options in observational research within natural settings.
www.ship.edu/~cgboeree/qualmeththree.html
There is a fun activity at the end where you are asked to observe and record your findings on 'an evening with friends'.

Activity 88 Designing a questionnaire/survey

Objective

To demonstrate the methodological problems that questionnaire/surveys can have and how these can be resolved.

Introduction

A questionnaire is a set of written questions that can be answered easily. It is especially useful in gathering information from large numbers of people. The construction of a reliable questionnaire is difficult because the slightest change in the way the questions are worded can completely change the result.

In a survey, research information is collected from a sample of people who are 'representative of the larger population'.

HOW DO YOU DO IT?

Write a short questionnaire (10–15 questions) on a topic of your own choosing and try it out on other students in your class.

Suggested topics might include:

- What causes stress?
- Why do people get angry?
- Why do people help others?
- What do people look for in a partner?
- Is behaviour affected more by your personality or the situation you find yourself in?

Class discussion:

- What has this experience taught you about constructing a questionnaire?
- How could you have modified the questions to improve your questionnaire?

Notes

Ideally, the research studies selected should be on a topic from the AS specification.

Homework

'Questionnaires have a number of advantages over interviews and are preferable for almost all research areas.' Discuss (200 words maximum).

Essential reading

Read the extract from Gross, McIlveen *et al.* (2000), page 150 'Asking Questions'.

Activity 89 Conducting interviews

Objective

To demonstrate the methodological problems that interviews can have and how these can be resolved.

Introduction

Interviews are becoming increasingly popular as a research tool. They have the advantage that they allow us to investigate people's experiences through the accounts that they give of those experiences. There are several types of interviews; the type chosen depends on the purpose of the research and the intended treatment of results.

HOW DO YOU DO IT?

1   For the following research topics decide which type of interview method is most appropriate. Give a reason for each answer:
  ● mothers' experiences of having a baby in hospital
  ● students' attitudes towards their old school
  ● an eyewitness account of a bank robbery
  ● a teenager recovering from anorexia nervosa
  ● people's views on a new chocolate bar.

2   Outline the problem with the following questions and rephrase them:
  ● What do you think of the new Russian language newspaper *The Daily Czar*?
  ● Do you think that not many people would not now understand the phrase BSE?
  ● Do you think that the press have become more biased and vindictive about the government since the Press Complaints Commission was strengthened?
  ● I suppose you know what is meant by the phrase 'zero tolerance'? Do you agree with it?
  ● Will you tell me everything you have ever learnt from sex education lessons in school and how it has influenced your subsequent behaviour?

3   Devise three fixed-choice questions for a structured interview about people's travel preferences (e.g. road, rail, bus etc.)

4   Devise three open-ended questions for a semi-structured interview about college students' experiences of taking A levels.

5   Think of some research topics where gender and ethnicity of the interviewer in relation to the interviewee could affect the research findings.

6   Give some examples of research where a social desirability in participants' responses might be anticipated. What is the term for this kind of bias in research?

7   If you were interviewing college students about their experiences of taking GCSEs, what problems and biases might you expect? What measures could you take to overcome these difficulties?

Notes

● Although interviews are a widely used research tool, they can be difficult to carry out well.
● The more unstructured the interview the more training the interviewer needs. Try to listen to the Radio 4 series *In the Psychiatrist's Chair* in which Professor Anthony Clare demonstrates the skills required to superb effect.

Homework

Imagine that you are going to interview your mother/father or guardian about their attitudes to parenting. Outline which interview method you would choose and produce five questions that you feel should be asked.

Essential reading

Read Gross, McIlveen *et al.* page 151, Table 7.2 to help with your answers.

Activity 90 Identifying the IV/DV and confounding variables

Objective

To identify what independent variable (IV), dependent variable (DV) and confounding variables are.

Introduction

The word 'variable' is used to describe something that alters when research is being carried out. The IV is the variable which is manipulated or altered in the research. The DV is the variable that is measured. Any change in the DV or result being measured should be *dependent* on the IV manipulation (hence the term *dependent* variable). Confounding variables are those which, if they are not controlled, might provide alternative explanations for why the dependent variable has altered during the study.

HOW DO YOU DO IT?

For the following research topics, suggest the most appropriate research method, write out a suitable experimental/alternative hypothesis, identify the IV and DV and outline how you would control for potential confounding variables.

- The reading abilities of a group of girls and boys were compared.
- A special new reading programme was given to a mixed group of boys and girls in order to compare it to the old reading programme used in the school.
- An investigation which looked into the relationship between smoking and lung cancer.
- The effect of sleep deprivation on memory was analysed.
- Whether a cognitive or a behavioural treatment programme was most effective in treating depression.
- A study into which is the more interesting subject, psychology or physics.
- The relationship between group size and conformity.

How could you improve (or check) the reliability and validity of your suggested studies? Distinguish between a confounding variable and an extraneous variable.

Notes

A correlation does not have an IV or DV. Some of the examples above are correlations!

Homework

Explain why a correlation does not have an IV or DV. What is the main drawback of a correlation? (50 words).

Essential reading

Read Gross, McIlveen *et al.* (2000), pages 144–146 to consolidate your knowledge.

Website reference:

http://www-personal.monash.edu.au/~psystats/p1stats/p1stats.htm
This includes first-year university lecture summaries from Monash University in Australia, on research design and analysis. Obviously, it goes into more detail than required for AS but it is well written and might be worth a look.

Activity 91 Ethics in psychological research

Objective

To understand some of the ethical factors associated with psychological research.

Introduction

Ethics are a set of moral principles outlining what is right and wrong. In terms of psychological research, they are the moral principles which guide research. Every psychological investigation is an ethical situation and therefore ethical issues must be addressed with all research. Research participants have rights and researchers have responsibilities and obligations. Although there are guidelines for research practices there is still room for debate and arguments as to what constitutes ethical or unethical research.

Materials

Overhead transparencies and pens, an overhead projector.

HOW DO YOU DO IT?

Working in groups, each group should find one research study to read and analyse. A list of some possible studies is given below (with Gross, McIlveen *et al.* (2000), page numbers) but you should not restrict your choice to this list:

- Ainsworth *et al.* (1978) 'strange situation' study (50–51).
- Watson & Raynor (1920) 'little Albert' study (103).
- Harlow (1959) rhesus monkey surrogate mothers (46).
- Brady (1958) 'Executive monkey' studies (778).
- Perrin & Spencer (1981) conformity study (120).
- Hofling *et al.* (1966) obedience in a hospital setting study (131).
- Zimbardo *et al.* (1973) prison simulation study (134).
- Darley & Latané (1968) New York subway helping study (776).
- Bandura Bobo doll study (243 and 512–513).

Each piece of chosen research could have been criticised for being unethical, although not all researchers would agree on this.

Each group should prepare an overhead transparency to present to the class, which should include:

- what the researchers were trying to test
- the IV and DV (if appropriate)
- the method that was used
- the findings and conclusion of the research.

On another transparency, each group should list all the possible reasons why their chosen research might have been considered unethical. All groups should then present their findings to the class.

In a class discussion, everybody should imagine that they are on a University Ethics Committee responsible for vetting and agreeing research topics. The class should vote on the studies covered earlier by each of the groups, deciding whether they should have been allowed to proceed and giving the reasons for their judgement. The class should agree a general list of ethical guidelines that they think should be in place before any research should take place.

Notes

Ideally, the research studies selected should be on a topic from the AS specification.

Homework

Get a copy of the British Psychological Society ethical guidelines (see the website below). Summarise these guidelines and compare and contrast them with the guidelines produced by your class (250 words).

Essential reading

Gross, McIlveen *et al.* (2000), pages 136–140 to consolidate your learning.

Website reference

www.bps.org.uk/charter/codofcon.htm

Activity 92 The BPS guidelines and general ethical principles

Objective

To introduce the BPS (British Psychological Society) guidelines and identify general principles associated with ethics in psychology.

Introduction

The ethics of any research project must be considered. The ethical and moral issues involved in psychological research are not simple ones. The American Psychological Association (APA) and British Psychological Association (BPS) produce their own set of guidelines which psychologists should adhere to. These are revised periodically. The key ethical issues involve informed consent, deception, debriefing and protection of participants.

Materials

Copy of BPS ethical guidelines (could be obtained through the Internet); pen and paper.

HOW DO YOU DO IT?

Consider the following questions:

- Is it ethical to deceive people taking part in an experiment as to its purpose? Can deception ever be justified?
- Is it ethical to expose people to stress or invade their privacy?
- Is it ethical to use groups of people, such as children, who are not in a position to give their informed consent?
- Is it ethical to deprive animals of stimulation, both in terms of immediate suffering and permanent damage?
- Is it ethical to cause great stress and possible permanent psychological injury to animals?

Go through the questions listed above and think of an example of at least one classic study which may be considered to violate each ethical consideration. Write up your work.
Use a different study for each one and think about whether the 'end justifies the means' in each case.

Notes

- Few questions of ethics are easily resolved, and often the investigator must weigh the question of scientific value against the rights of the subject.
- You should also refer to Critical Issue, *Ethical issues in psychological research* in 12.1 Social Influence Topic.

Homework

'Psychology doesn't need a set of ethical guidelines. The problem with such guidelines is that they either restrict interesting avenues of research or psychologists merely try to push the limits of the guidelines. Either way they are a hindrance to the science of psychology.' Discuss this view (200 words maximum).

Essential reading

Read Gross, McIlveen *et al.* (2000), pages 136–140 and pages 773–777 to help with your answers.

Website reference

http://www.ukc.ac.uk/psychology/handbooks/ethics/bps.htm
A comprehensive extract from the British Psychological Society ethical principles guidelines for participants (1997).

Activity 93 Analysing qualitative data

Objective

To understand the nature and use of qualitative research in psychology.

Introduction

There are broadly two types of data collected in psychology: quantitative and qualitative. Quantitative data is perhaps the most common and best known and tends to lend itself more to statistical analysis. However, qualitative data is becoming increasingly accepted amongst some psychologists and may be better suited to certain research areas. Content analysis refers to an approach which reduces qualitative data to a quantitative form. The activity outlined below uses content analysis.

Materials

You will need to photocopy two 'lonely hearts' columns from different papers. The *Saturday Times* and *Private Eye* are good ones to use.

HOW DO YOU DO IT?

Groups of two need to skim read both of the 'lonely hearts' newspaper articles. You must decide whether to compare male and female adverts or adverts from the two different newspapers. Choose 20 adverts from each paper, selected at random, to analyse. Write, in your own words, any general differences you note between the two papers or gender-related adverts. Are there any obvious patterns?

Try to identify key criteria within each of the adverts. These might include:

- income/financial status
- education
- attractiveness/photo
- religion
- socio-economic group
- humour.

You may want to categorise the adverts into what the people writing them are seeking and what they are offering. You could devise a series of tally charts for each characteristic you have identified and count the number of adverts which fall into each category.

For example, if you wanted to see if men were seeking attractiveness in a potential partner more than women you could produce the following summary table. At a glance, a table such as this summarises the qualitative information in a quantitative way.

Attractiveness	Seeking	Offering
Males	10	2
Females	3	9

Carry out further analyses like this, using different categories and see if you find any pattern to the adverts.

Write up your findings and use quotes to illustrate your answers.

You will be asked to report briefly on your findings in class.

Notes

Qualitative research forms the basis of a new approach in psychology. The method used in understanding one's subjective view of the world is likely to remain a controversial area and represents a real challenge for contemporary psychology.

Homework

Compare and contrast quantitative and qualitative research methods . What are some of the advantages and disadvantages of each? Why are qualitative methods often regarded as more 'ecologically valid'? (200 words maximum.)

Essential reading

- Gross, McIlveen *et al.* pages 170–172.
- See also *Psychology Review* articles Vol. 2, No. 2, pages 13–15 and Vol. 6, No. 2, pages 20–21 (published by Phillip Allan) for further information on qualitative research methods.

dispersion: a quick test

Objective

To understand the appropriate use of measures of central tendency and dispersion.

Introduction

For any set of data, a 'measure of central tendency' is a representative or typical value. The mean, the median and the mode are the most commonly used measures of central tendency.

A measure of dispersion is a single figure which summarises how 'widely spread', or dispersed, are the data *values*. The range and the standard deviation of a set of data are the most commonly used measures of dispersion.

HOW DO YOU DO IT?

Fill in the missing words from the sentences below. The missing words all relate to measures of central tendency or dispersion.

Read the relevant pages from your textbook and then try to fill in the words, without looking up any information. (Warning: the same word can appear more than once!)

1 The .... is calculated by adding up all the scores in a given condition and dividing by the number of participants in that condition.
2 The .... is the value which occurs most frequently in a data set.
3 The .... is the middle value in a data set when the values have been rank ordered.
4 The .... is the sum of the scores divided by the number of values.
5 The .... is used at the ordinal level on ranked data.
6 The .... is used at the interval level on measured values.
7 The .... is the most appropriate central tendency measure for nominal data (in categories).
8 The .... is most sensitive to all values.
9 The .... is greatly affected by extreme values in one direction and by skew.
10 The .... and .... may not be actual values in the data set, whereas the .... must be.
11 The .... is the simplest data measure and is unaffected by a few extreme scores.
12 The formula for the .... is top value - bottom value +1.
13 One problem with the .... is that you do not know how spread out the scores are within the ....
14 The distance of a score from its group mean is known as its ....
15 Roughly .... per cent of all values fall between one standard deviation below and above the mean.

Notes

You do not need to know *how* to calculate the standard deviation but *you must* know *what it is* and *what it means*.

The answers to this test can be found on page 171.

Homework

Copy into your file and learn Table 7.12 on page 165 of Gross and McIlveen *et al.* (2000).

Essential reading

Gross and McIlveen *et al.* (2000); pages 164–166 'Measures of dispersion and central tendency'.

Activity 95 Levels of measurement

Objective

To understand the different types of measurement levels.

Introduction

Before a set of data can be analysed, it is necessary to know the level of measurement that applies to the data. The level of measurement determines the amount of information contained in the data and this will guide decisions about the most appropriate methods of representing and analysing the data. Levels of data include: **n**ominal, **o**rdinal, **i**nterval and **r**atio. Some psychologists use the acronym NOIR to remember this. Nominal is the least detailed with interval and ratio data providing the most information.

HOW DO YOU DO IT?

With which level of measurement would you associate each of the following?

- the time taken for a reaction test
- marital status of an adult
- time taken to run 100 m
- the star ratings for hotel standards
- level of distress shown by a patient
- the number of students who play sport regularly
- placing in a 100 m race
- the number of boys and girls doing psychology
- the position of a pop song in the top 20 chart
- the number of copies each artist has sold in the top 20
- placing of a skater for 'artistic expression'
- temperature in degrees Fahrenheit
- the weights of people's brains.

Think of a further three examples for each data type: nominal, ordinal and interval and ratio. Imagine that we want to measure the following abilities/behaviours using three different types of data: nominal, ordinal and ratio. Outline how you would do this for:

- intelligence
- marathon running ability
- car driving ability
- eyesight
- football skills.

Notes

There is not always unanimous agreement amongst psychologists and statisticians as to what represents true interval or ratio data. An IQ score is obtained from an IQ test which has been standardised. However, are two people with the same IQ score of exactly equal intelligence when, inevitably, they will have answered different questions correctly? One psychologist might answer 'no' and call IQ data ordinal data, whereas another might answer 'yes' and count it as ratio data. In practice, examiners would have to credit either answer. This highlights the fact that even in statistics there are still things to argue about!

Activity 96 Which graph?

Objective

To understand the appropriate use of histograms, bar charts, frequency polygons and scattergraphs.

Introduction

It is always useful to be able to draw an appropriate graphical representation of your data. A correctly drawn graph enables a reader to see immediately any pattern or trend in the data. There are many different types of graph, each with their own uses. The most common ones are histograms, bar charts, frequency polygons and scattergraphs.

Materials

Graph paper.

HOW DO YOU DO IT?

- Summarise the distinguishing features of a bar chart, frequency polygon, histogram and scattergraph.
- Draw the most appropriate type of graph for each of the following (completely fictitious) data tables.

Table 1

Driver gender	Driver age	Accident frequency (per 10 000 km)
Male	Less than 25 years	8
	Over 25 years	4
Female	Less than 25 years	6
	Over 25 years	3

Table 2

Scores of psychology students in first psychology test (max 10)
4 5 3 8 7 7 7 9 8 7 6 4 2 3 4 3 4 7 6 5 3 2 2 4 6 7 7 6 4 3 2 4 5 6 6 4 5 4 8 5 1

Table 3

Scores of psychology students in first psychology test (max 10)
4 5 3 8 7 9 7 7 1 8 7 6 4 2 3 4 3 4 7 6 5 3 2 2 4 6 7 7 6 4 3 1 4 5 6 6 4 5 4 8 5

Scores of psychology students in last psychology test (max 10)
7 6 3 2 1 9 7 8 10 8 10 6 7 7 5 6 3 4 8 8 7 5 6 6 4 10 7 9 6 7 3 7 4 1 6 9 4 6 4 9

Table 4

Participant (hours per week)	IQ score	Amount of homework completed
1	125	10
2	115	8
3	130	11
4	98	1
5	103	5
6	106	6
7	130	2
8	135	10
9	126	8
10	101	4
11	119	9
12	143	8
13	108	3
14	121	6
15	125	7
16	111	4

Homework

For each graph above, describe your findings in two or three sentences. Use descriptive statistics such as mean, median, mode, correlational trend where appropriate.

Essential reading

Gross, McIlveen *et al.* (2000), pages 166–170, paying particular attention to, 'Some important points about statistical charts'.

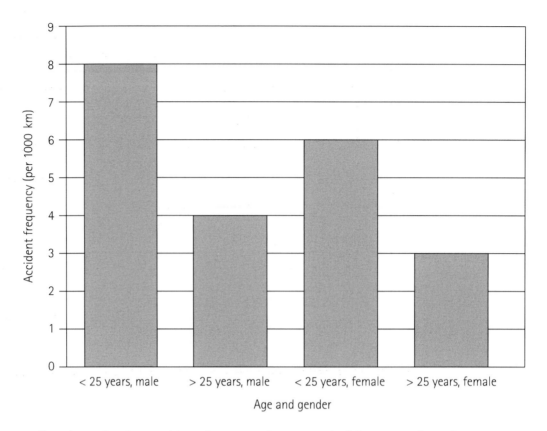

Bar chart showing accident frequency (per 1000 km) by age and gender

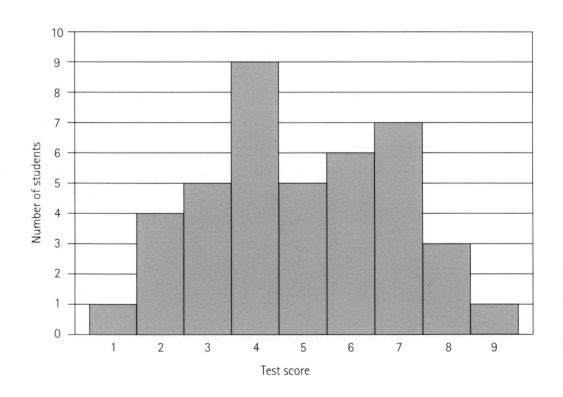

Histogram showing psychology student test scores

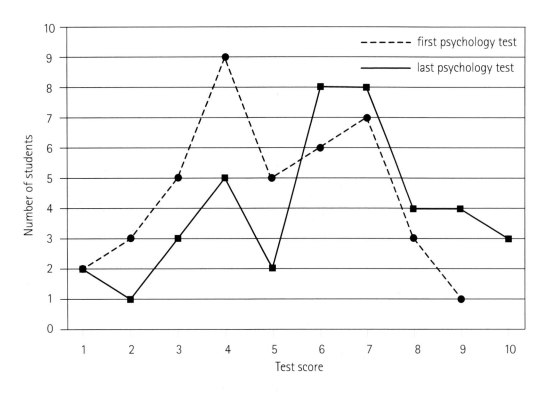

Frequency polygon showing psychology student test scores (first and last tests)

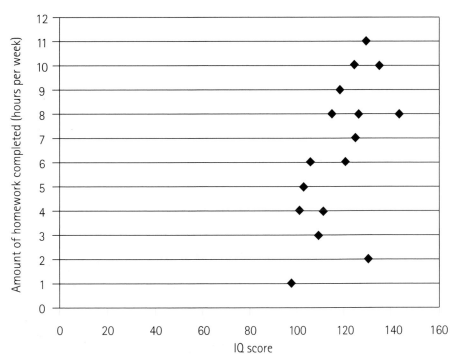

Correlation showing IQ score against amount of homework completed (hours per week)

Activity 97 Designing and carrying out an investigation

Objective

To design and conduct an investigation in psychology.

Introduction

To carry out successful research, many factors need to be carefully considered from the design stage through to implementation and data analysis. This activity gives students an opportunity to progress through all these stages and carry out a full investigation of their own choosing.

Materials

Depend on the investigation chosen.

HOW DO YOU DO IT?

You will be asked to get into groups of two or three and design a practical activity based on one of the research methods below. Some suggested topics for each research method are included.

Laboratory experiment
The effect of drinking coffee (caffeine) on reaction times.
The effect of words and images on memory recall.
Does listening to Mozart enhance problem solving ability?

Field experiment
Will more women drivers than men stop at a zebra crossing for a pedestrian?
Are women less likely to walk under a ladder (i.e. more superstitious) than men?
Who gets helped the most, men or women? (Male and female experimenter needs to drop a pile of books.)

Natural experiment
Are women car drivers more compliant than male drivers?
Do more women return library books on time than men?
Are people who play team sports more sociable than those who don't?

Correlational analysis
Does the amount of violent television watched correlate with aggressive behaviour?
Does the number of days absent from school correlate with exam performance?
Is there a correlation between couples' IQ levels?

Naturalistic observations
Are women car drivers more compliant than male drivers?
Is there a gender difference in the aggression of schoolchildren?
Is there sex-role stereotyping in British television adverts?

Questionnaire surveys/interviews
Do smokers and non-smokers differ in their attitudes to smoking?
What do people look for in a partner?
Which factors determine a student's subject choices at AS/A level?
(Groups could investigate the same issues and see whether the research method used affects the results collected.)

- Fill in a project brief form (your teacher should have a copy). Check with your teacher that your design is feasible and ethical.

- Conduct the investigation and collate the raw data. 'Eyeball' the data and draw a results summary table. This might include the mean, mode, median and so on.
- Draw a graph/chart which best illustrates your data.
- You will be asked to present your research design and findings to the rest of the group.
- State some limitations of your chosen design and suggest ways in which your chosen design might have been improved.

Notes

This activity could be used as part of the Key Skills Level 3 in Communication or might be developed as A2 coursework.

Activity 98 Revision summary sheet

1 Define each of the following research methods and outline three advantages and three disadvantages of each.
   - laboratory experiments
   - field experiments
   - natural experiments
   - correlational analysis
   - naturalistic observations
   - questionnaire surveys
   - interviews.

2 Explain and give an example of:
   - experimental/alternative hypothesis
   - null hypothesis
   - one-tailed (directional) hypothesis
   - two-tailed (non-directional) hypothesis.

3 Describe the difference between independent, repeated and matched pair experimental designs.

4 Understand how participants are selected including the use of random sampling.

5 Explain and give an example of:
   - independent variable
   - dependent variable
   - confounding variable
   - extraneous variable.

6 What is a pilot study and why are they used?

7 Distinguish between reliability and validity.

8 What is:
   - internal validity
   - external validity
   - ecological validity.

9 What is content analysis?

10 List some of the arguments for and against the use of qualitative research techniques.

11 Define what the following are, and when they might be most appropriately used:
   - mean
   - mode
   - median
   - range
   - standard deviation.

12 Distinguish between nominal, ordinal, interval and ratio data and cite an example of each.

13 Define and give an example of a negative correlation and a positive correlation.

14 Ensure you know when the following would be used and what they look like:
   - histogram
   - bar chart
   - frequency polygon
   - scattergraph.

Activity 99 Research methods multiple choice test

1 An experiment:
   a involves the researcher manipulating the independent variable to see the effect on the dependent variable
   b cannot be used to infer cause and effect
   c is the least scientific method used in psychology
   d always has an independent variable, but does not need a dependent variable.

2 Field experiment is:
   a a study where the experimental method occurs in a more naturalistic setting
   b where an experiment takes place in a field
   c where there is no manipulation of the IV and the experiment takes place in a natural setting
   d where a researcher observes people in a natural setting.

3 An alternative hypothesis:
   a is the opposite of the null hypothesis
   b is the opposite of the experimental hypothesis
   c is another term for experimental hypothesis and is the alternative to the null hypothesis
   d is the opposite of a one-tailed experimental hypothesis.

4 A correlation:
   a measures the strength of the relationship between two variables
   b can infer cause and effect
   c involves the manipulation of a DV on an IV
   d cannot be described by a numerical value.

5 An independent variable:
   a measures the extent to which people display independent behaviour
   b is a variable that is not involved in an experiment; the variable is thus independent of the experiment
   c is manipulated by the researcher to see whether a change occurs in the dependent variable
   d is the variable that is measured by the researcher.

6 Independent measures design:
   a involves two groups, matched across separate conditions
   b uses the same participants in both conditions
   c tests different participants in each condition
   d is where each participant takes part in all conditions.

7 An experimenter wants to investigate the effects of caffeine on sleep patterns. In this experiment:
   a the amount of sleep is the dependent variable and caffeine is the independent variable
   b the amount of sleep is the independent variable and caffeine the dependent variable
   c both are independent variables
   d both are dependent variables.

8 We want to find the IQ of students at your college. We place all students names into a hat and draw out 100 for testing. This is known as:
   a stratified sampling
   b biased sampling
   c random sampling
   d skewed sampling.

9 If we find a correlation coefficient of -0.90 between reaction time and alcohol consumption, it means that:
   a as alcohol consumption increases, reaction time increases
   b as alcohol consumption increases, reaction time decreases
   c alcohol consumption causes reaction time to increase
   d as alcohol consumption decreases, reaction time decreases.

10 Demand characteristics refer to:
   a aspects of a study where participants guess what is expected of them and act accordingly
   b where a participant demands to know the results of a study
   c a situation where unrealistic demands are made of participants
   d the list of standardised instructions making demands on the participants.

11 Qualitative data involves:
   a analysing data using numbers and frequencies
   b the researcher estimating the quality of the research
   c an independent researcher judging the quality of a given piece of research
   d looking at data from the point of view of the meanings and implications they have.

12 The median:
   a always has the highest value
   b is affected by an extreme abnormal value
   c is the most common value in a given data set
   d is the sum of the values, divided by the number of values.

13 The mean:
   a always has the highest value
   b is unaffected by an extreme abnormal value
   c is the most common value in a given data set
   d is the sum of the values divided by the number of values.

14 The mode:
   a always has the highest value
   b is affected by an extreme abnormal value
   c is the most common value in a given data set
   d is the sum of the values divided by the number of values.

15 For the following seven scores, 5, 6, 7, 8, 9, 10, 12:
   a the median is 8
   b the mean is 8
   c the mode is 7
   d a and b are true, but not c.

16 Systematic sampling involves:
   a selecting participants on a random basis, such as by drawing names out of a hat
   b stopping people in the street randomly
   c choosing participants who are available
   d selecting every nth person from a list.

17 The marks for artistic expression that skaters get in a competition constitute:
   a nominal data
   b ordinal data
   c interval data
   d ratio data.

18 Which is the least detailed type of data:
   a nominal data
   b ordinal data
   c interval data
   d ratio data.

19 Confounding variables, if not controlled:
   a do not affect the dependent or independent variables
   b might provide alternative explanations of why the dependent variable changed in an experiment
   c are ignored by the experimenter
   d are produced by observer bias.

20 A double-blind experiment is:
   a where neither the data gatherers nor the participants know which condition they are in
   b the participants are kept blindfolded during the experiment
   c when the participants are unaware of the condition they are in, but the data gatherers do know
   d where the participants blindly guess the purpose of the experiment and act accordingly.

Answers to Activity 94

   1 Mean
   2 Mode
   3 Median
   4 Mean
   5 Median
   6 Mean
   7 Mode
   8 Mean
   9 Mean
   10 Mean, median, mode
   11 Mode
   12 Range
   13 Range, range
   14 Deviation
   15 68 per cent

Answers to Activity 99

1 a
2 a
3 c
4 a
5 c
6 c
7 a
8 c
9 b
10 a
11 d
12 c
13 d
14 c
15 d
16 d
17 b
18 a
19 b
20 a

7   *Key Skills*

Introduction

Key skills are generic skills that are useful for people to perform well in education, training and life in general. They help people to become integrated and useful members of the work force and help them to benefit from life-long learning.

The main key skills are:
■ Communication
■ Application of number
■ Information technology (IT).

The wider key skills are:
■ Working with others
■ Improving own learning and performance
■ Problem solving.

Each key skill is available at four levels (1–4) of increasing difficulty.

It appears likely that many schools and colleges will concentrate on achieving the key skills in the three main areas and this chapter concentrates exclusively on these and aims at level 3. This does not mean students' responses demonstrating achievement at other levels cannot be rewarded.

There are two components which make up the scheme of assessment for each of the main key skills. These are an internally assessed portfolio of evidence and an externally assessed test. The internally assessed evidence will be externally moderated. Each school or college should have one or more key skills co-ordinators who may be asked for advice at any time and who also ensures internal standardisation at the school/college.

Opportunities for key skills delivery depend on a number of factors including subject specification, teaching strategy and availability of resources. Not every key skill has to be delivered through each subject specification. On the following pages there are some suggestions as to ways in which key skills can be delivered. We suggest that it might be best to deliver one key skill in communication through the specification. We provide detailed help on how to do this. We suggest that the other key skills can be covered to a greater or lesser extent through the coursework component in A2. These are only suggestions, and teachers are ideally placed to decide where their own students can produce evidence as part of their key skills portfolio.

Website reference

Further details about key skills are available at:
http://www.QCA.org.uk/nq/ks/com_app_it2.asp.

Communication key skills

Communication is the key skill which we have identified as being the easiest to deliver through Psychology Specification A.

To attain Level 3, students have to:
■ C3.1a Contribute to a group discussion about a complex subject.
■ C3.1b Make a presentation about a complex subject, using at least one image to illustrate complex points.

- C3.2 Read and synthesise information from two extended documents about a complex subject.
- C3.3 Write two different types of documents about a complex subject. One piece of writing must be an extended document (at least three pages) and include at least one image.

The communication key skill could be delivered through one tailor-made and carefully targeted exercise, such as that outlined on the following three pages (which are directed to the student) on the 'Individual differences' sub-section, or through numerous, diverse exercises across different modules covered as and when appropriate.

Covering communication through an entire topic (in this case, Module 11.2 'Individual differences: abnormality') has a number of advantages:
- planning is easier and more manageable
- all work is completed at the same time so deadlines can be set for the entire class
- marking and moderation are easier, since all the work is on the same topic.

Note

Care must be taken with the 'Individual difference' module, particularly with regard to the critical issues of anorexia nervosa and bulimia nervosa as students may have some first-hand experience of the area.

On the following pages, activities are outlined which should enable students to achieve communication key skill at level 3 and at the same time cover much of the material for Module 11.2 'Individual differences: abnormality'.

Individual Differences: Abnormality

11.2a	Defining psychological abnormality
	• In terms of statistical infrequency, deviation from the norm and a 'failure to function adequately'
	• Limitations of these definitions (including cultural relativism)
11.2b	Biological and psychological models of abnormality
	• Assumptions of biological (medical) model and implications for treatment
	• Assumptions of psychodynamic model and implications for treatment
	• Assumptions of behavioural model and implications for treatment
	• Assumptions of cognitive model and implications for treatment
Critical issue	Eating disorders
	• Clinical characteristics of anorexia nervosa
	• Explanations and research studies on anorexia nervosa
	• Clinical characteristics of bulimia nervosa
	• Explanations and research studies on bulimia nervosa

General textbooks

1 Gross, R. and McIlveen, R. (1998) *Psychology: A New Introduction*. Hodder & Stoughton
2 Gross, R. and McIlveen, R. (2000) *Psychology: A New Introduction* 2nd edition. Hodder & Stoughton
3 Gross, R. (1996) Psychology: *The Science of Mind and Behaviour* 3rd edition. Hodder & Stoughton
4 Hill, G. (2001) *AS Psychology through Diagrams*. Oxford University Press

Advanced reading

1 Davison, G. and Neale, J. (1994) *Abnormal Psychology* (6th edition) New York: Wiley

Web addresses

See page 114 in Gross (1996), No. 3 in the list above.
Please notify staff of any useful web addresses you find for future help.

Individual Differences: Abnormality

Incorporating Communication Key Skill Level 3

Introduction

In this module, we are going to cover the material by using a self-supported form of open learning which also has the benefit of covering all the aspects required for the communication key skill level 3 criteria listed below. You must:

C3.1a	Contribute to discussions
C3.1b	Make a presentation
C3.2	Read and synthesise information
C3.3	Write different types of document

Further details of the key skills can be downloaded from the QCA website (http://www.qca.org.uk/key skills)

■ You will achieve all these criteria, by preparing a talk/presentation on ONE of the topics listed in the table below.

■ You will need to research your topic. There are various sources you could use, such as textbooks, handouts provided by your teacher, past issues of psychology journals, and the Internet. You should use your key skills assessment sheet C3.2 to help you keep a detailed record of references used and a bibliography. You must use two or more extended documents (more than three sides of A4), one of which must include an image.

■ Once you have obtained sufficient material, you will need to prepare a presentation on your allocated topic to present to the rest of the class. This talk should last at least six to ten minutes. You must ensure that you fulfil all the requirements for C3.1b when completing this presentation. (See your assessment sheet for C3.1b for details)

■ To achieve C3.1a you must be involved in a discussion on your chosen topic area, and fulfil all the necessary requirements for this. Your topic for discussion should follow on from your presentation. It may include an evaluation of the approach, or a controversial issue linked to the approach.

■ You should provide your teacher with a list of questions which might be asked of you following your presentation.

■ The talk might be videotaped as evidence that you have met the criteria for key stage 3 communication. This is not compulsory – assessment sheets should be enough to provide the evidence required.

■ As a result of your research and presentation, you should produce two written documents – one of which should be three sides or more. These could include things like a handout to go with your talk, a summary of key points for your discussion, an essay, a report, etc. At least one of these documents should include one or more images (graphs, charts, pictures or tables with statistics) that adds to the understanding of your information.

■ At the end of this activity, you MUST have pieces of evidence to include with all your assessment sheets. Read the key skills sheets (3.1–3.3) carefully so you know what kind of evidence to collect. Here are some examples of the kind of things that may be counted as suitable evidence:

■ Photocopies of textbooks, journal articles, Internet pages – annotated or highlighted to show which bits you have selected and used:
  ■ a comprehensive reference and bibliography list
  ■ a copy of the text/prompt cards used in your talk

- overhead transparencies used in the talk
- drafts and final versions of your written documents showing where corrections and changes have been made
- a summary of points you put forward in your discussion.

You must also ensure your assessment sheets for C3.1a, C3.1b, C3.2 and C3.3 are filled in, attached to the relevant evidence and submitted to your teacher for assessment. You must keep all this documentary evidence in order to show to the assessors who award key skills. Without this evidence, you will not pass. It is your responsibility to do this and it must be kept in college.

Extended reading articles which you might choose to use

- Davison G. & Neale J. (1994) *Abnormal Psychology*, 6th edition, pages 449–453, Wiley & Sons. Chichester, UK.
- Gross, R.D. & McIlveen, R. (1998) *Psychology: a new introduction*, pages 613–619, Hodder & Stoughton, UK.
- Cardwell, M, *et al.* (2000) *Psychology for A level* (2nd edition), pages 98–105, Collins Educational.
- Eysenck, M & Flanagan, C. (2000) *Psychology for AS level*, pages 183–194, Psychology Press, E Sussex, UK.
- Cox, E. (2000) P*sychology for AS level*, Oxford University Press, Oxford, UK.

What you should keep in your key skills folder

- Photocopies of extended articles, annotated and highlighted in the relevant places.
- Evidence of any earlier draft versions with changes/amendments you have made.
- The final version of your extended document.
- Overhead transparencies from your talk.
- The handout you produced for your talk (this will be your other written document).
- A list of questions that were asked after your talk and how you managed the ensuing discussion.

Title of possible topics

	Topic	Name
1	Defining abnormality in terms of statistical infrequency, deviation from social norms, 'a failure to function adequately' and deviation from ideal mental health. Limitations associated with these attempts to define psychological abnormality (including cultural relativism).	
2	Assumptions made by biological (medical) model of abnormality. The biological (medical) model's view regarding the causes of abnormality. The implications for treatment for those who adopt the biological (medical) model of abnormality.	
3	Assumptions made by psychodynamic model of abnormality. The psychodynamic model's view regarding the causes of abnormality. The implications for treatment for those who adopt the psychodynamic model of abnormality.	
4	Assumptions made by behavioural model of abnormality. The behavioural model's view regarding the causes of abnormality. The implications for treatment for those who adopt the behavioural model of abnormality.	
5	Assumptions made by cognitive model of abnormality. The cognitive model's view regarding the causes of abnormality. The implications for treatment for those who adopt the cognitive model of abnormality.	
6	The clinical characteristics of anorexia nervosa. Explanations of anorexia nervosa in terms of the psychodynamic model of abnormality, including research studies on which these explanations are based.	
7	The clinical characteristics of anorexia nervosa. Explanations of anorexia nervosa in terms of the behavioural model of abnormality, including research studies on which these explanations are based.	
8	The clinical characteristics of anorexia nervosa. Explanations of anorexia nervosa in terms of the cognitive model of abnormality, including research studies on which these explanations are based.	
9	Explanations of bulimia nervosa in terms of the biological (medical) model of abnormality, including research studies on which these explanations are based.	
10	The clinical characteristics of bulimia nervosa. Explanations of bulimia nervosa in terms of the psychodynamic model of abnormality, including research studies on which these explanations are based.	
11	The clinical characteristics of bulimia nervosa. Explanations of bulimia nervosa in terms of the behavioural model of abnormality, including research studies on which these explanations are based.	
12	The clinical characteristics of bulimia nervosa. Explanations of bulimia nervosa in terms of the cognitive model of abnormality, including research studies on which these explanations are based.	

• Your teacher will help explain these talks and guide you in the preparation and searching for material.

Application of number, level 3

To attain level 3, students have to cover the following requirements:

N3.1	Plan and interpret information from two different sources, including a large data set
N3.2	Carry out multi-stage calculations to do with: a amounts and sizes b scales and proportions c handling statistics d rearranging and using formulae You should work with a large data set on at least one occasion
N3.3	Interpret results of your calculations, present your findings and justify your methods. You must use at least one graph, chart and one diagram

N3.1 *Plan and interpret information from two different sources, including a large data set*

This could be covered in the planning of the coursework. It is anticipated that students choose two different research papers to use as a basis for their own investigation and ensure that the papers include data and statistics from a large data set. The students' introduction in their coursework and the project brief form can be used as evidence of this. Photocopies of the original papers may be kept as additional evidence.

N3.2 *Carry out multi-stage calculations to do with:*

a amounts and sizes
b scales and proportions
   This could be covered in the method section of the coursework. Students could use a specific sampling method to outline the proportion that their sample represents compared to the wider population. In addition, they could analyse the different proportions and ratios within their sample (e.g. males to females, left-handed to right-handed, and so on) providing that this is relevant to the purpose of the study. In the results section, students could use descriptive statistics to demonstrate which proportion of students achieved a given result. This might be expressed in percentage terms of those students, say, above or below the mean and it could, of course, depend on the condition that they were in. Again, such data analysis would have to be relevant to the study.

c handling statistics
d rearranging and using formulae
   This could be covered in the results section of the coursework. Students need to ensure that they have a large data set of 50 items or more. Carrying out the appropriate statistical analysis on this data should provide the necessary evidence. Carrying out the statistical analysis by hand and demonstrating the step-by-step use of formulae is desirable.

N3.3 *Interpret results of your calculations, present your findings and justify your methods. You must use at least one graph, chart and one diagram*

This could be covered in the results section and part of the discussion section of the coursework. Students will need to summarise their data in a descriptive form, using an appropriate chart, graph or diagram. It might be worth including a summary table of the results. Again, students will need to justify their choice of descriptive statistics, graphs or charts and statistical calculations. In either the results section or the discussion, students will need to explain the results that they obtain and relate them back to their original aims and alternative/experimental hypothesis and accept or reject it accordingly. Justification of the research method (PB3 and PB4) and statistical analysis (PB7) on the project brief form can also be used as additional evidence for the portfolio.

Information technology, level 3

To attain level 3, students have to cover the following requirements:

IT3.1	Plan and use different sources to search for, and select, information required for two different purposes.
IT3.2	Explore, develop and exchange information and derive new information to meet two different purposes.
IT3.3	Present information from different sources for two different purposes and audiences, including at least one example of text, one example of images and one example of numbers.

IT3.1 *Plan and use different sources to search for, and select, information required for two different purposes*

This could be covered by students when they select information from two different sources such as the Internet, journals, newspapers, CD-ROM or Psychology Review. They would need to use these sources as preparation for different purposes, such as an essay, short answer questions or for the introduction to their coursework. Students could include the original sources and the finished material as evidence. Screen prints of search engines and the relevant pages would be useful. Students must justify their choice of material and assess it for relevance and quality.

IT3.2 *Explore, develop and exchange information and derive new information to meet two different purposes*

This could be covered through the use of MS Word, Excel or Access. Students need to show evidence that they have accessed information either through the Internet or, even better, through the use of e-mail, to investigate a particular psychological topic. This could include e-mailing a psychology department or an individual lecturer to confirm data or ask a question about a specific topic. Students could present the information gathered using IT in different ways, such as an advertisement for participants, a newspaper report on a study, or a letter to an ethics committee complaining about a particular study they have researched. All of these documents should demonstrate their use of IT and include such things as headers and footers, page numbers, newspaper columns, mail merge and so forth where appropriate.

It should be possible for students to use a spreadsheet to create descriptive statistics for their coursework. Students need to show how the data have been manipulated using absolute and relative values and appropriate use of formulae.

IT3.3 *Present information from different sources for two different purposes and audiences, including at least one example of text, one example of images and one example of numbers.*

This could be covered through two presentation documents suitable for their purpose and the targeted audience. For example, a student might wish to present to their peers material which was obtained from the Internet in the form of an edited essay or a revision help sheet. Students could produce a poster presentation of their coursework to show to the class. The best examples could be used for classroom displays. The documents must include one example of text, one example of an image and one example of numbers. Students also have to show that they can develop the structure and content of the presentation material by providing appropriately annotated, older versions of the work.

Students should also be able to use Powerpoint as part of a presentation to satisfy all of the requirements for level 3. Students would have to keep evidence of each stage of the process they followed to their final presentation.

Note

As you can see, we recommend that the communication key skill be covered within the Psychology AS Specification. Coursework which is part of the A2 Specification can be used to cover the other key skills (IT and application of number). It is strongly recommended however that you consult with your college or school key skills internal moderator at all stages (planning, implementation and assessment) when working with key skills to ensure that the work produced meets all of the standards and requirements.

Students also have to take a written exam in each of the three main key skills. Examples of written tests are available at www.qca.org.uk

8   *What to Do After the AS Exam: Producing Coursework*

The most obvious answer is to relax and unwind ready for the summer holidays! However, in reality, the AS exam is likely to be at the beginning of June and this means that students will have a number of lessons at the end of their first year prior to starting the A2 course in the second year. Of course, many centres may start the A2 course immediately, but the problem arises that students may not know whether they plan to continue with Psychology at A2 until they receive their results in the summer. This would mean that teachers may have students in their class who are still undecided as to whether they intend to continue with psychology at A2 level and may therefore not be very committed to the course in those final weeks.

One solution is to conduct the coursework component of A2 at this time. There are a number of benefits to this:

- It should prove an enjoyable exercise for all the students, who will be able to put into practice research skills that they have already learned for AS Module 3.
- Students can learn transferable skills which will be of use even if they ultimately decide they do not wish to study psychology at A2 level (e.g. scientific report writing, data collection and analysis).
- Students can be asked to write up their coursework over the summer (this may also act as a 'filtering' process for A2 student suitability).
- Students may meet many of the criteria needed to cover the main key skills (level 2 or 3).

There follow sections on:

- what coursework is and what needs to be done for the A2 assessment
- some suggested titles for coursework
- help on how to write up coursework
- a coursework checklist.

What coursework involves and what needs to be done for the A2 assessment

Objectives:

- to give direct experience of some of the methods used by psychologists to collect and analyse data
- to understand the difficulty encountered when carrying out research and the problems associated with interpreting results and drawing conclusions from these results.

Introduction

Progress in science depends on active communication between research workers in the same, and in related, fields. It is therefore essential to describe the results of empirical research as accurately and as effectively as possible. Some general advice on writing experimental reports is given below, including some of the conventions which apply to scientific reporting.

Replicability is essential in scientific enquiry. In principle, it should be possible for someone else to exactly repeat your experiment from your description alone. Report writing skills are one of the main skills that psychologists have to learn.

Purpose of a coursework write-up

Put simply it is the place in which you tell the story of your study, specifically:

- what was done
- why it was done
- what was found
- what it means.

This should be done clearly and concisely. The aim is to be explicit and avoid ambiguity without, of course being too verbose! The reader will then be able to repeat the study in all its essential procedural features. Quite often, different research units report quite similar studies which yield different results. To work out why this happened one needs full information about *what* was done. If you regard replicability as your goal, you will succeed with your coursework write-up.

Remember: when in doubt spell it out!

Setting out your report

There is no single, correct way to set out all scientific reports. Scientific journals vary in their format, and you will find that different members of academic staff have their own preferences as regards presentation. In many cases it would be foolish to impose a rigid format, since for some areas of our discipline this could be quite impractical. Therefore the format suggested below should be taken as a general guide. If you divide your report into sections and give them clear headings, with numbering where appropriate, you will assist the reader (and the marker) to understand your report without difficulty. You will not necessarily get everything right first time, but don't despair. One of the best ways to acquire a feeling for report writing is to read articles in learned publications such as the *British Journal of Psychology, The Journal of Experimental Psychology*, and so on.

Basic structure:	Title
	Abstract
	Introduction
	Method
	Results
	Discussion
	References
	Appendices

A2 Requirements

Candidates must produce ONE piece of coursework drawn from any area of the AS or A2 specification.

Data can be collected and analysed in groups of four candidates or fewer but the write-up must be each individual's own work. The appropriate method can be one of those covered in the specification, namely: laboratory, field and natural experiments, surveys, observational studies and correlational research. The results must involve appropriate inferential statistics.

Candidates must complete a project brief form before starting any data collection to check that ethical guidelines are being adhered to and to help with their planning of the coursework. Marks are awarded for the project brief form up to a maximum of 12 marks. Copies of the psychology project brief proposal forms are available from AQA.

Suggested titles for coursework:

Here are some suggested titles for coursework. Always be aware of ethical issues and associated safety issues when approaching participants.

Developmental psychology

Due to the greater likelihood of ethical issues arising with this module, AQA advises that candidates should not select investigations from this area. However, some possible suggestions include:
- Is there sex-role stereotyping in British television adverts?
- Can Piagetian conservation experiments be replicated/modified?
- Is there a correlation between self-estimated IQ and gender and/or self-esteem?

Individual differences

Again, this module is likely to have serious ethical issues implications, so care must be taken over the choice of an investigation from this area. However, one possible suggestion is:

■ Is there an association between fear rating and experienced trauma? (A questionnaire study.)

Social psychology

■ Who get helped the most: men or women? (Male and female experimenter need to drop a pile of books.)
■ Are women car drivers more compliant than male drivers?
■ Will more women drivers than men stop at a zebra crossing for a pedestrian?
■ Does the amount of violent television watched correlate with aggressive behaviour?
■ Do smokers and non-smokers differ in their attitudes to smoking?
■ What do people look for in a partner?
■ Does the order of presentation of positive and negative traits affect overall personal evaluation?

Physiological psychology

■ Does a placebo affect vigilance of psychomotor tasks? (Caffeine can be used as an apparent stimulant; both groups consume decaffeinated coffee, only one group is told that they have drunk caffeine).
■ Does invasion of personal space affect pulse rate?
■ Do pheromones/scent affect pulse rate? Some perfumes/aftershaves use pheromones (e.g. musk oil).
■ Do relaxation tapes work? Relaxation tapes versus white noise; measure pulse rate or galvanic skin response to assess level of relaxation/stress.
■ Is there evidence of circannual rhythms (e.g. birth dates) in humans?
■ Does grooming hair affect pulse rate or galvanic skin response? (In some animals it is supposed to be relaxing – is it the same in humans?)

Cognitive psychology

■ Does listening to Mozart enhance problem solving ability?
■ Does self-esteem affect the time taken to extract embedded figures (hidden shape located within a complex figure)?
■ Does perceptual set affect participants' interpretation of Leeper's lady?
■ Is perception of the 'moon illusion' affected by context (e.g. with or without horizon)?
■ Are words or images remembered best?
■ Does context affect memory recall?
■ Do 'leading' questions affect eyewitness testimony?
■ Is there a correlation between STM capacity and age in children? STM capacity increases until age of 11 when 'magic seven' is reached.
■ Is it true that the more bizarre the image the better the recall?
■ Are high schema expectancy items recalled better than low expectancy items? People recall items they expect to see in certain situations (e.g. desk in classroom) – these are high expectancy items. They are less likely to remember items not found in a given situation.
■ Is it easier to recall 'doodles' which are given an explanation or not? It is suggested that nonsense drawings are better recalled if they are given a thematic label which explains them.
■ Is recall affected by the state one is in during learning and subsequent recall? Test of state dependent recall. Does current mood dictate recall of memories matching mood?
■ Sleep and memory – is interference greater after a day's activity or a night's sleep? Does sleep help to consolidate memory?
■ Does using a story to link unrelated words improve recall? (Use of narratives to aid recall of word lists.)
■ Does similarity of interference tasks affect recall?
■ Do a balancing task and reading use the same central processor? (Manual balancing task for each hand whilst 'shadowing' prose. Do these two tasks draw on resources

from the same processor? If so, reading aloud using the right hand to balance a rod will be harder than using the left hand and reading aloud.)
- Recall of word lists versus picture lists whilst shadowing prose. Again, are there separate processors for different inputs/sense modalities? If so, recall of pictures will not be affected by shadowing, whereas learning and recall of words will (caution: proper controls needed because images are better remembered than words).

Comparative psychology

A visit to the local zoo may be needed here!
- Is there a dominance hierarchy in any herd species? (e.g. horses, zebras.)
- Is there a pecking order when feeding? (Based on age, weight, size, breeding, etc.)
- Do certain primates favour particular hands?
- Do individuals in larger groups spend less time scanning? Group size and vigilance (scanning behaviour) either in humans or non-humans.
- Is it possible to show latent learning in rodents?
- Is there an optimum group size for communication? (Optimum group size in humans is three, therefore communication should be greatest in groups of this size.)
- Do friends co-operate more than strangers? Or males more than females? Use the 'Prisoner's dilemma' strategy game.

How to write your coursework

The report should be similar to a journal article. The report write-up should be no longer than 2000 words, excluding tables, figures and appendices. It is usual to write up coursework in continuous prose, in the past tense and to avoid colloquialisms. The report should have the following sub-headings:

Title

This should be precise enough to give the reader a good idea of the topic you are investigating.

Table of contents

This is optional, but is best included along with page numbers.

Abstract (approximately 150 words)

This is a summary of your coursework and tells the reader whether it is worth reading any further! Obviously, the examiner will read on regardless. The Abstract should include approximately two sentences from each of the other sections in your report: the theoretical background, the aim and hypothesis, the design method and participants, a brief outline of the results, the conclusion, and suggestions for future research. Although the abstract comes first it is usually best to leave its writing to the end.

Introduction (approximately 600 words)

This answers why you carried out the study. It should include general theoretical background, identifying the main theories, controversies and investigations of the chosen topic. It is important to concentrate on relevant material. This section is very much like a 'funnel' starting off with a broad perspective and leading on to the more precise aims and hypotheses under study.

Aims

The overall aim of the study should be set out here.

Hypotheses

The precise experimental/alternative hypothesis should be included, along with the null hypothesis. These should be as precise and unambiguous as possible. A justification of the direction of the hypothesis should be included (i.e. one-tailed or two-tailed). The minimum acceptable level of significance should be stated, this is normally 5 per cent ($p \leq 0.05$).

Method (approximately 600 words)

This covers what you did. All details of the method should be reported so that other researchers can replicate the study if they wish to. Materials used in the study such as questionnaires, observation checklists and standardised instructions, should be included in the appendices. The method is split into several sub-sections.

Design

There are no hard and fast rules about what goes in the design section and what goes in the procedure section. The design section should cover:
- the choice of method such as laboratory experiment, observation and so on
- the type of design you used (e.g. repeated/independent measures or matched pairs)
- the choice of observational technique, if applicable (e.g. time or event sampling)
- the identification of variables such as the independent variables, dependent variable (if applicable) and confounding variables
- ethical considerations.

Participants

This is where you describe your sample. The sub-section should cover:
- the target population described in terms of relevant variable such as age, gender, socio-economic groups and so on
- the method you used to obtain your sample, e.g. random, opportunity, and so on
- the actual sample in terms of how many participants there were, how they were selected and recruited and described in terms of any relevant variables outlined above
- how participants were allocated to conditions.

Apparatus/materials

This section should include a description of any technical equipment involved and how it was used. The main point of this section is relevance. Only include materials that are directly relevant to the investigation, not trivial inclusions such as 'pencil and paper' (although this may be crucial to some studies!) Include relevant mark schemes for any tests or questionnaires in the appendix.

Standardised procedure

The aim of this section is to allow precise replication of your study. It is a step-by-step description of exactly how your study was conducted. Describe what happened in the order it happened. Details of where the study took place, standardised instructions and debriefing should be included. If the instructions are lengthy, it may be better to place them in an appendix. Try not to repeat information that has appeared elsewhere in your method section.

Controls

Sometimes this information is included in the design section. Controls to be mentioned would include counterbalancing, random allocation of participants to groups, single- or double-blind procedures, control of extraneous variables and steps taken to avoid bias in the sampling or experimental procedures.

Results

This covers what you found and is also a crucial section, since it presents the data you have collected and needs to be presented so that others can evaluate your work. The section should be written in connected prose with the support of tables and/or figures (graphs) which are referred to in your text. The main features of this section are described in more detail below.

There is an art to tabulating your data. If you organise yourself fully before you run your study, there should be no need to write out your raw data more than once. Do not insert it in the body of the text, but possibly in an appendix. Tables and figures in the text will typically be very abbreviated, or summary versions of the raw data. Each summary table should be clearly headed.

Do not include any names of the participants in answer sheets or on questionnaires and so forth. Names should be treated as confidential information. One example answer sheet, questionnaire and so on should be included in the appendix.

Descriptive statistics

Descriptive statistics are essential and give the reader a chance to 'eyeball' the data. You should try to summarise your results in the most appropriate graphical form. You could include numerical statistics such as measures of central tendency (mean, mode or median) or measures of dispersion (range, standard deviation). Your aim must be to present the key findings in the most straightforward manner. Sometimes the choice of graphical presentation is a difficult one. Label tables and figures clearly so that the reader understands what inserted values represent (always specify measurement units), and number these tables and figures so that they can be easily referred to in the text. Tables should be numbered and titled above the table, figures and graphs below. Labels on graph axes should be unambiguous. Do not include too much information. Indicate the sample size. Make sure the figure makes optimum use of the space available. Join points on line plots with straight lines and not meandering curves. Treat figures (graphs, histograms, etc.) as aesthetic products (not easy perhaps!) Do not label figures or tables 'Figure to show ...'. Use a simple but informative title about the variables displayed. Describe the key features briefly in the text, where appropriate. Do not provide both a table and a figure of the same data; this is wasteful of time and space, so decide which works best.

Inferential statistics

When statistical tests or analyses on the data are conducted, you should state clearly why you chose a particular test and what it tests for. This should be in terms of whether the data involves repeated or independent measures or correlational data. Calculations should not appear in the body of the text but should be shown clearly in an appendix so that a reader can follow them easily if necessary. Be clear about the outcome of the statistical analyses. In the main text, summarise the key findings and cite test statistics. You should include a statement on the observed and critical table values of the test, the significance level and whether the test was one-tailed or two-tailed. You must show that you understand what the results of your statistical tests mean. Do the results mean that you accept or reject your null hypothesis? Do not attempt to interpret the results at this stage; leave that to the discussion section.

Discussion (approximately 600 words)

This explains what you think the results mean. In AS the discussion section is worth the most marks and is split into four sub-sections (which are marked as such).

Explanation of findings

This must begin with a clear description of the key findings. The findings should be stated in psychological terms, in relation to the aims and hypotheses identified earlier. What bearing do your findings have upon the original hypotheses? State what your most important finding is and explain what this illustrates. All results are results. You must never ignore or dismiss findings that do not fit with previous findings. Science would not progress if scientists dismissed any finding that they were not looking for. Your purpose is to show why you obtained the results you did and what they show. A good researcher will themselves act as a participant before conducting a study. Alternatively, you may have conducted a pilot study. This should give you insight into the study and reports by the participants themselves can be most informative. Often they give information about possible sources of error in the design or procedure. Also, participants tend to adopt different strategies, changing course in the middle of a study. They may not do what you want or expect them to do and such information can be included in the discussion section, either here in the explanation of findings sub-section or the limitations and modifications sub-section.

Relationship to background research

This is where you account for and discuss your results in terms of previous research findings. You should refer back to the relevant research studies mentioned in your introduction. Mention any aspects of your design that may account for any differences between your findings and those of previous studies. If your results support previous reviewed work, this section may be quite short, although it is still worth emphasising any design or procedural differences that there may be.

Limitations and modifications

Do not sidestep embarrassing findings or paradoxical results. If the study 'went wrong' try to locate possible sources of error. These might include measurement techniques, poor sampling, lack of controls and/or poor procedures. Even the best designed study is likely to have some flaws or suggest better ways of conducting the study. Outline what was done, what was intended (this may not be the same) and how things might have been improved or modified.

Implications and suggestions for further research

Questions to consider in this section include:

- If you were to repeat the study, would you alter the methodology in any way, and why?
- What further experiments are suggested to you by this experiment and its findings?
- Can you think of better ways of testing the hypotheses?
- Do you think that standard studies in the literature might be improved?
- Are there any other applications or implications that arise as a result of your findings?

When making suggestions for further research, only do so if they arise directly out of your results. Try to be precise with your suggestions and do not make general statements such as 'A lot more work needs to be done in this area'. Specific suggestions, such as using more participants, eliminating confounding variables (e.g. background environmental noise) and improving standardised instructions are fine provided you have demonstrated that some of these factors have affected your findings in some way.

Conclusion (approximately 50 words)

Finally, you might end this section with a paragraph which recapitulates the key findings and conclusions which can be drawn from the study.

References

You should cite *only* authors' names and dates of publications which are in the text. You should list *all* references that you have cited in the text. The purpose of a reference list is to enable others to research the references, so if in doubt, give as much information as possible.

Use the following standard format for your list of references:

- **Journal articles:** author's name(s) and initial(s), year of publication (in brackets), title of article (lower case preferred), title of journal (in full preferably in italics), volume number, page numbers.

  For example:
  Shepard, R.N. and Metzler, J. (1971) Mental rotation of three dimensional objects. *Science*, 171, 701–703.

- **Books:** author's name(s) and initial(s), year of publication (in brackets), title of book (initial capitals for key words all in italics), publisher, place of publication.

  For example:
  Bartlett, F.C. (1932) *Remembering: A study in Experimental and Social Psychology.* Cambridge University Press, Cambridge.

■ **Chapters in books:** combine aspects of the above methods by giving the author of the chapter and his/her chapter title first followed by 'In A. Smith (ed) ...', etc.

For example:
Cohen, G. (1982) Theoretical interpretations of visual asymmetries. In J.G. Beaumont (ed), *Divided Visual Field Studies of Cerebral Organisation*. Academic Press, London.

Appendices

You should provide appendices containing the full instructions given to subjects, the raw data, and calculations for statistical analyses. In addition, if you have generated lists of words or other stimulus materials for use in your study they should be included as an appendix. The different information should be put in numbered appendices so that you can refer to them easily in your text. This is not a rough work section and all information should be presented clearly and unambiguously. It is perhaps unfortunate that such sections do not usually appear in published journal articles.

General considerations and style

This kind of report writing is somewhat specialised. Clear and lucid descriptions are required, while unsupported personal opinions and over-generalisations must be avoided. Only those conclusions warranted by your results should be drawn, and where speculations are made this should be made clear to the reader. You should write in connected prose throughout the report, *never* let it degenerate into a series of notes. It is preferable to write in the third person, past tense. This, along with many of the other points made in these notes, tends to be a convention of scientific writing. Try to avoid slang, stereotyped phrases; these are often vague and ambiguous. However, reports *do* require imagination and creativity; they need not be dull and tedious. Remember that it is doubtful that we ever 'prove' anything in psychology. Results may support a hypothesis, but 'prove' is definitely a word to avoid.

Are you completely confused?

If you have never written up a practical before reading this it will probably be confusing or even terrifying. Do not worry, these notes have been produced to help you. Read them through a few times before you write your coursework report and discuss them with other members of the class.

A2 Level psychology coursework checklist

Before you start your coursework, you should fill in the psychology project brief proposal form.
This checklist is designed to help with the details required in a coursework write-up. Follow the order of items in each section. Required length is 2000 words.

(Mark allocations are shown in brackets)

TITLE
A short, precise title, but more than three words. [ ]

A CONTENTS
All pages numbered. [ ]
    Contents listed in appropriate scientific style. [ ]

B ABSTRACT (3)
    Aim of the investigation. [ ]
    One sentence about one relevant research. [ ]
    Method: e.g. experiment/observation? [ ]
    Independent design/repeated measures? [ ]
    Sampling: e.g. opportunist/random? [ ]
    Participants: number, age and gender. [ ]
    Independent and dependent variables (if relevant). [ ]
    Result (including values of statistical analysis). [ ]
    Level of significance (e.g. P = 0.05). [ ]
    Experimental or alternative hypothesis. [ ]
    Hypothesis accepted or rejected. [ ]
    Final sentence: implication for behaviour. [ ]

C INTRODUCTION (10)
C1 **(5)** Background psychological literature. [ ]
    Relevant research discussed. [ ]
C2 **(3)** Background linked to the aims with [ ]
    reasons and some detail of method. [ ]
C3 **(2)** Experimental/alternative hypothesis. [ ]
    Null hypothesis. One or two-tail test? [ ]

D METHOD (4)
D1 Design
    Experiment/observation/questionnaire? [ ]
    Independent design/repeated measures? [ ]
    Explanation of the design. [ ]
    Independent and dependent variables (if relevant). [ ]
    Extraneous variables. [ ]
    Removing bias e.g. counterbalancing. [ ]
    Any assumptions to be stated. [ ]
    Conventional level of significance such as 0.05. [ ]
D2 Participants
    Target population. [ ]
    Sampling, e.g. opportunist/random. [ ]
    Age range. [ ]
    Numbers of each gender. [ ]
    Allocation to conditions. [ ]
    Did any decline or drop out? [ ]
    Naïve. [ ]
D3 Materials
    Description and explanation. [ ]
    Refer to appendix page number. [ ]
    Diagram of materials and location (if necessary). [ ]
D4 Procedure
    Explain the investigator's role. [ ]
    Describe the participant's role. [ ]
    Consent from and briefing of the participants. [ ]
    Standardised instructions (refer to appendix page). [ ]
    Debriefing of, and thanks to, the participants. [ ]

E RESULTS (8)
E1 **(4)** Draw up a summary table of data. [ ]
    State result with calculated and critical values. [ ]
    Level of significance (0.05).
    Number of participants. [ ]
    Give basic facts from graph/s (e.g. range). [ ]
    State in which appendix the raw data is listed
    and where the statistical analysis is found. [ ]
    Give a full justification of the choice of test. [ ]
E2 **(4)** Raw data in appendix (labelled). [ ]
    Pooled data (where applicable in the appendices). [ ]
    Relevant tables with full headings. [ ]
    Statistical analysis in full (in appendix). [ ]
    Relevant graph/s: frequency plot of raw data/ [ ]
    bar chart/scattergram/pie chart, etc. [ ]
    Check headings and labels. [ ]
    Analysis of graphs (e.g. trend/range of responses). [ ]

F DISCUSSION (12)
F1 **(3)** Outcome in terms of hypotheses including [ ]
    result, critical value and level of significance. [ ]
    Comment on the graphs related to the result. [ ]
F2 **(3)** Result linked to background literature and
    research that agrees or disagrees with this result. [ ]
    Be specific and quote research names from C1. [ ]
F3 **(3)** Possible sources of error. [ ]
    Include any uncontrolled variables. [ ]
    Be critical of any design fault. [ ]
    Limitations (actual and possible). [ ]
    Corresponding modifications. [ ]
F4 **(3)** Implications of further research. [ ]
    Possible gender/age/cross-cultural issues. [ ]
    Suggestions thoroughly discussed. [ ]
    Research in terms of everyday behaviour. [ ]

CONCLUSION
    Key findings and conclusion. [ ]

REFERENCES (2)
    Sources quoted in conventional style (in handbook). [ ]
    Include all research names mentioned in C1. [ ]
    In alphabetical order of surnames. [ ]
    Include statistical textbook and computer package. [ ]

APPENDICES
    Number and title each appendix. [ ]
    Diagram of materials/apparatus if relevant. [ ]
    Standardised instructions. [ ]
    Copy of test/questionnaire/survey. [ ]
    Raw data/pooled data.
    Statistical analysis in full (manual or StATPak). [ ]
    Graph/scattergram/pie chart (Supastat or Excel). [ ]

    Reporting style (past tense, no pronouns). [ ]
    Quality of language (use 'spellcheck' and
    check 'by hand'). [ ]

Psychology Specification A: AS Mark Scheme

The specification consists of six modules, all of which are compulsory. These are tested in three examination units. These are:

Unit 1   Two structured questions on cognitive psychology. Candidates must answer one.
Two structured questions on developmental psychology. Candidates must answer one.
This unit lasts one hour.

Unit 2   Two structured questions on physiological psychology. Candidates must answer one.
Two structured questions on individual differences. Candidates must answer one.
This unit lasts one hour.

Unit 3   Two structured questions on social psychology. Candidates must answer one.
Two structured questions on research methods. Candidates must answer both.
This unit lasts one hour 15 minutes.

Each unit contributes 33.3 per cent of the AS level (16.67 per cent of the total A level marks).

Assessment objectives

The assessment objectives (AO) are the same for all units. They are:

AO1 (Assessment Objective 1)	This involves knowledge and understanding of psychological material (e.g. theories, terminology, concepts, studies and methods) including the effective communication of this knowledge.
AO2 (Assessment Objective 2)	This involves the analysis and evaluation of psychological material (e.g. theories, terminology, concepts, studies and methods) including the effective communication of this knowledge.

There is also A03, covered mainly through the coursework component in A2 but some of this is covered in the second question in research methods, which is a 'design a study' question which aims to assess a candidate's ability to conduct research.

Quality of written communication (QoWC): the marks are the same for all units. They are:

2 marks	The material contains accurate and clear ideas, a broad range of technical and specialist terms and only minor errors in spelling, punctuation and grammar.
1 mark	The material contains reasonable expression of ideas, a reasonable range of technical and specialist terms and few errors in spelling, punctuation and grammar.
0 marks	The material contains poor expression of ideas, limited use of technical and specialist terms and poor spelling, punctuation and grammar.

Marking allocations

Each AS question is worth 30 marks. AO1 attracts 18 marks and AO2 attracts 12 marks. Students have to complete two questions per unit.

QoWC offers two marks for each unit. Thus each unit is marked out of 62.

The marking allocations tend to be similar for each question with the same mark allocations. In summary, these are as follows:

AO1

Six mark questions	Three mark questions	Mark allocation
5–6 marks	3 marks	The description is accurate and detailed.
3–4 marks	2 marks	The description is generally accurate but less detailed.
1–2 marks	1 mark	The description is lacking in detail and may be muddled and/or flawed.
0 mark	0 mark	The description is inappropriate, incorrect and/or irrelevant.

AO2

12 mark questions	Mark allocation
11–12 marks	There is informed commentary, thorough analysis of the relevant psychological material and it has been used in a highly effective way.
9–10 marks	There is informed commentary, reasonably thorough analysis of the relevant psychological material and it has been used in an effective way.
7–8 marks	There is a reasonable commentary, slightly limited analysis of the relevant psychological material but it has been used in an effective way.
5–6 marks	There is a reasonable commentary, limited analysis of the relevant psychological material but it has been used in a reasonably effective way.
3–4 marks	There is superficial commentary, rudimentary analysis of the relevant psychological material and there has been minimal interpretation of this.
1–2 marks	There is a just discernible commentary, analysis is weak and muddled and the material presented may be irrelevant.
0 marks	The commentary and any analysis is wholly irrelevant to the question.

Most commonly with research methods there are two mark or three mark allocations as follows:

Two or three mark questions	Marking allocation
2–3 marks	Accurate and informed description or explanation.
1 mark	Brief or muddled answer.
0 marks	Incorrect or inappropriate answer.

For more detailed help, please refer to the document available from AQA entitled Psychology Specification A: Specimen units and Mark schemes.

Some examples of the format of the AO1 questions are:

'Describe one study …'(6 marks)
'Describe one theory …' (6 marks)
'Describe two factors which explain …' (3 + 3 marks)
'Give two criticisms of …' (3 + 3 marks)
'Describe two differences between … and …' (3 + 3 marks)
'Describe one research study that has investigated …' (6 marks)
'Describe two research studies that have investigated …' (3 + 3 marks)
'Explain what is meant by the terms … and …' (3 + 3 marks, or 2 + 2 +2 marks if three terms are asked)
'Describe the procedures and findings of one study that has …' (6 marks)

'Outline the procedures used in one study of ... and give one criticism of this study' (3 + 3 marks)

Some examples of the format of the AO2 questions are:
'A relevant quote. To what extent has psychological research ...' (12 marks)
'Evaluate research into ...' (12 marks)
'A relevant quote. Evaluate the extent to which ...' (12 marks)
'A relevant quote. Assess the extent to which ...' (12 marks)

When a quotation is used, it does not have to be explicitly addressed in the candidate's answer.

Psychology Specification A

Unit 1: Cognitive Psychology and Developmental Psychology

Time allowed: one hour In Section A, answer ONE question. In Section B, answer ONE question.	**Information** Mark allocations are indicated in the paper. A maximum of two marks can be awarded for quality of written communication.

Section A: Cognitive Psychology

Answer one question from this Section.
Answer all sections of the question you chose.

1a   Explain what is meant by the terms 'encoding' and 'chunking' in relation to STM. (3 + 3 marks)

  b   Describe the main features of the multi-store model of memory proposed by Atkinson & Shiffrin. (6 marks)

  c   Describe the aims and conclusions of one study of face recognition. (6 marks)

  d   Assess the extent to which Freud's ideas on repression enable us to explain forgetting. (12 marks)

2a   Describe two differences between STM and LTM. (3 + 3 marks)

  b   Describe the procedure and findings of one study that has investigated the nature of forgetting in long term memory. (6 marks)

  c   Describe one model or theory of memory. (6 marks)

  d   '*EWT remains the best form of evidence available for jurors in order to determine guilt or innocence.*'
     To what extent has psychological research found EWT to be unreliable? (12 marks)

Answers to Section A: Cognitive Psychology

Marking criteria: refer to the tables at the start of this chapter for the precise mark allocations.

Question 1

  a   Encoding or chunking involves the transformation of sensory input into a form which allows it to be entered, or registered, into memory. Chunking involves integrating smaller units of information into larger 'bits' in order to increase STM capacity. Our capacity to read is largely based on chunking of letters into words, words into phrases and phrases into sentences.

  b   Answers should include descriptions of the three memory stores: sensory, short-term and long-term and the way information flows between them. Concepts such as rehearsal and forgetting should be included. A diagram of the multi-store model would probably help.

  c   Appropriate studies could include Bahrick et al. (1975), Buckhout (1974), Bahrick (1984). Note that the answer should concentrate on the aims and conclusions of the study rather than the procedure and/or findings.

  d   It is relevant to point out that experimental studies of repression are ethically questionable and that the clinical case study method used by Freud has been questioned. However, studies by Lewinger & Clark (1961), Parkin (1993) and Kaminer & Levine (1991) with people suffering 'post-traumatic stress disorder' provide relevant evaluative evidence. Alternative arguments for forgetting can also be proposed, provided that candidates contrast the evidence for these with that of repression.

Question 2

  a The differences could be outlined in terms of capacity, duration of storage, coding or the effects of brain damage (retrograde and anterograde amnesia).

  b The study must relate to long-term memory and might cover availability: trace decay (e.g. Jenkins & Dallenbach 1924) or interference theory, or accessibility (cue-dependent or context dependent memory) or repression.

  c A description of any the following models would be appropriate: the multi-store model, working memory model or levels of processing model.

  d Answers might include an evaluation of reconstructive memory (Bartlett) and mention might be made of the accuracy of flashbulb memories. Loftus' research could be included to demonstrate the extent to which EWT is unreliable in terms of misleading post-event information including the use of language (Loftus & Palmer 1974). The validity of Loftus' research could also be included and the applicability of such memory research studies. The key point is that candidates must analyse and evaluate psychological research.

Section B: Developmental Psychology

Answer one question from this Section.
Answer all sections of the question you chose.

  3a Explain what is meant by secure and insecure attachments. (3+3 marks)

  b Outline the procedures used in ONE study that has investigated individual differences in attachments and give ONE criticism of this study. (3+3 marks)

  c Outline Bowlby's maternal deprivation hypothesis. (6 marks)

  d *'Psychologists disagree sharply about the developmental effects of day care.'*
   Assess the extent to which research supports the view that day care has negative effects on children's cognitive and/or social development. (12 marks)

  4a Explain what is meant by the terms 'attachment' and 'deprivation' in relation to child development. (3+3 marks)

  b Describe the procedures and findings of ONE research study that has investigated the long-term effects of deprivation OR privation. (6 marks)

  c Give TWO criticisms of the study you have described in part b. (3+3 marks)

  d *'According to some theories all humans are born with basic needs and drives such as hunger and thirst and it is the process of satisfying these that leads to the formation of attachments in infants.'*
   Consider the extent to which psychological theories have been successful in explaining attachments. (12 marks)

Answers to Section B: Developmental Psychology

Marking criteria (refer to the tables at the start of this chapter for precise mark allocations)

Question 3

  a Securely attached infants show distress at their mother's absence and on reunion are quickly reassured. Such infants tend to have sensitive mothers and are more confident to explore. They manage their emotions with strangers nearby. Insecurely attached infants tend to have insensitive mothers. Such infants if anxious-resistant, are insecure with their mother and distressed if she leaves. If the infant is anxious-avoidant then indifference is shown towards their mother. Research on rhesus monkeys could be made relevant.

  b The episodes in the 'strange situation' by Ainsworth et al. (1978) illustrate individual differences in attachment. Observations were made on the infant's reaction to the mother's separation and reunion with a stranger present. Lamb et al. (1985) criticised the study for being highly artificial, limited in quantitative data and in failing to take account of the mother's behaviour. Criticism may be levelled at interpretations of findings in a cultural context.

  c According to Bowlby, if separation occurred between mother and infant during the critical period (i.e. the first three years) there can be serious and permanent harm to development. This might include: aggressiveness, delinquency, dependency anxiety, affectionless psychopathy, intellectual retardation, social maladjustment, depression and dwarfism.

d Bowlby argued that a child whose mother goes out to work experiences maternal deprivation. This has been supported and challenged by different research. Belsky & Rovine (1988) supported Bowlby and used the 'strange situation' but this was considered inappropriate for children in day care. Other research shows day care does not weaken attachment to the mother, for example, Schaffer (1996), Scarr (1998) and Clarke-Stewart (1991). Other findings suggest children are worse, cognitively and socially, if mothers start work too early (Baydar & Brooks-Gunn, 1991). Other results have been neutral (Horwood & Fergusson, 1999). Further comments could be made about the longitudinal character of the research and unrepresentative university day care centres used.

Question 4

a Attachments are intense, enduring emotional ties between a child and a specific person. The first crucial attachment usually involves the mother–child relationship. Kagan *et al.* (1978) described it as 'an intense emotional relationship that is specific to two people, that endures over time.' Deprivation is the separation of the child from the attachment figure. In relation to child development there can be short-term effects of distress or long-term effects of separation anxiety.

b Earlier studies have included long-term effects of maternal deprivation, for example, Goldfarb (1947); Spitz & Wolf (1945) and Bowlby (1946). Later research by Rutter (1970) and Tizard & Hodges (1989) has studied privation. Relevant non-human animal research, for example Suomi & Harlow (1977), could be cited.

c Methodological questions can be raised, for example: type and size of sample and ethical considerations. Issues of causation, replication and retrospection could be used. The practical application of research would be a positive criticism.

d Freud's psychoanalytical 'cupboard love' theory could be a starting point. The behaviourist view supports the argument that infants become attached to those who satisfy their physiological needs. Harlow's studies with rhesus monkeys challenged both of these explanations. Mere description of a theory will only receive limited credit and the question expects comment on their success at explaining attachments. Schaffer & Emerson (1964) emphasised the relevance of multiple attachments. Ethologists, such as Lorenz, argued that an imprinting-like process was involved in attachment. Bowlby believed that infants display a strong innate tendency to become attached to one particular adult female (monotropy), which was qualitatively different to all other attachments.

Psychology Specification A

Unit 2: Physiological Psychology and Individual differences

| Time allowed: one hour
In Section A, answer ONE question.
In Section B, answer ONE question. | Information
Mark allocations are indicated in the paper.
A maximum of two marks can be awarded
for quality of written communication. |

Section A: Physiological Psychology

Answer one question from this Section.
Answer all sections of the question you chose.

1a   Outline two sources of stress in the workplace. (3 + 3 marks)
   b   Describe the procedures and findings of one study into the relationship between stress and coronary heart disease. (6 marks)
   c   Describe how gender can play a role in how people respond to stress. (6 marks)
   d   *'On the basis that stress almost certainly plays a role in at least some illnesses, it is important to find ways in which it can be managed and its impact on health minimised.'* Consider the effectiveness of psychological approaches to stress management. (12 marks)

2a   Describe one research study relating to life changes as a source of stress. (6 marks)
   b   Describe one physical method of managing stress. (6 marks)
   c   Describe the main features of the general adaptation syndrome. (6marks)
   d   *'When an individual believes that an unpleasant event can be predicted, modified or terminated, it is less likely to be perceived as stressful.'* Assess the role of control in the perception of stress. (12 marks)

Answers to Section A: Physiological Psychology

Marking criteria: refer to the tables at the start of this chapter for the precise mark allocations.

Question 1

   a   Answers could refer to job uncertainty, work overload/underload, interpersonal relationships. Alternatively answers could include aspects of the work environment such as temperature, noise or overcrowding. More detailed answers will include an example or description.
   b   The most likely study to be included is Friedman & Rosenman (1974), the Western Collaborative Group Study which found that Type A personality types were twice as likely to develop heart disease as non-Type As. Note that the answer should focus on the procedure and findings rather than aims and conclusions.
   c   The work of Frankenhauser (1983, 1991) can be used to explain the role of socialisation into gender roles and how this may affect our biological response to stress. Answers could include reference to the work on Type A/B behaviours, and that women are less likely than men to be Type A personalities probably because Type A behaviour patterns reflect the traditional male gender role.
   d   Psychological approaches include relaxation and meditation, stress inoculation training (Meichenbaum 1976) and increasing 'hardiness' (Kobasa 1977). Answers should include briefly the aim, rationale and procedure of each method selected and focus mainly on the effectiveness of the method. Empirical evidence should also be included.

Question 2

a The most likely study to include is the Holmes & Rahe (1967) social readjustment rating scale. Having assigned numerical 'stress values' to events that people often experience at some time in their lives they found that those individuals who had experienced an unusually high number of stressful events in a given period were more likely to suffer prolonged illness in the following year than people who had not.

b Answers could refer to the use of drugs or biofeedback. The answer should include the aim, a rationale and procedure for the chosen method.

c The answer should include the name of each stage: the alarm stage, the resistance stage, the exhaustion stage, and a brief description of the physiological response during each stage.

d Empirical evidence in this answer could, for example, include Rotter's (1966) locus of control, Glass & Singer's (1972) study showing that mere knowledge of control could reduce perceived stress, and the distinction made by Wadew & Tavris (1993) between primary and secondary control. Methods of managing stress may be discussed in terms of how they help an individual gain a sense of control.

Section B: Individual differences

Answer one question from this Section.
Answer all sections of the question you chose.

3a Explain what is meant by the 'statistical infrequency' definition of abnormality and give one limitation of this definition. (3 + 3 marks)

b Outline two assumptions made by the psychodynamic model in relation to the causes of abnormal behaviour. (3 +3 marks)

c Describe one research study into the causes of anorexia nervosa. (6 marks)

d 'Research has suggested that eating disorders are unlikely to be explained by a single cause.' Evaluate two models of abnormality in terms of their explanation of anorexia nervosa. (12 marks)

4a Describe two attempts to define psychological abnormality. (3 + 3 marks)

b Describe two assumptions made by the biological model of abnormality. (3 + 3 marks)

c Outline the implications of the cognitive model for the treatment of abnormal behaviour. (6 marks)

d To what extent have psychological definitions of abnormality failed to take into account cultural differences? (12 marks)

Answers to Section B: Individual differences

Marking criteria: refer to the tables at the start of this chapter for the precise mark allocations.

Question 3

a According to this definition, behaviour that is statistically infrequent within a population is regarded as abnormal, whereas frequent behaviours are regarded as normal. Those who focus on the statistical aspect of abnormal behaviour measure specific characteristics of individuals, for example IQ or personality traits, and the distribution of these within the population. One such population distribution is the 'normal distribution curve' which depicts the majority of people as being in the middle (or average) as far as any particular characteristic is concerned, with few people falling at either extreme. Therefore an assertion that a person is normal implies that he/she does not deviate much from the average in a particular trait or behaviour pattern.

One limitation of this definition is that it overlooks the importance of the desirability of behaviours. It is assumed that behaviours that are infrequent (abnormal) are undesirable and potentially harmful to the individuals concerned. However, there are some behaviours which are so common as to be normal in the statistical sense, but which are regarded as constituting psychological disorder. Examples are depression and anxiety. Likewise, there are some abnormal/statistically infrequent behaviours which are desirable, for example high IQ.

b The psychodynamic model assumes that abnormal behaviour is the product of some form of unconscious conflicts that stem from childhood. For Freud this was seen in the dynamics of the id, ego and superego. The role of the ego is to reconcile the opposing forces of the id and superego. When conflict is excessive, defence mechanisms come into operation, however these cannot be used indefinitely. Once the defence mechanisms become overused, abnormal behaviour is exhibited. A second assumption concerns the role of early childhood experiences. The source of the unconscious conflicts lie in childhood.

c The study must relate to the causes of anorexia nervosa, and must include details of the aims, participants, procedures, results and conclusions (which should relate back to the aims).

For example, Holland *et al.* (1984) investigated the claim that anorexia nervosa had a genetic cause by studying the concordance rate of twins. The concordance rate refers to the likelihood of both twins developing anorexia nervosa. If there was a purely genetic link, it would be expected that there would be a concordance rate of 100 per cent. Holland *et al.* (1984) studied 30 pairs of female twins, with at least one twin having been diagnosed with anorexia nervosa. They found that if a monozygotic (identical) twin suffered from anorexia nervosa there was a 55 per cent chance that their twin would also suffer. When this is compared to the concordance rate of 7 per cent that was found for dizygotic (non-identical) twins it can be seen that genes must play an important role as monozygotic twins share all the same genes.

d You could choose any two of the following: biological; behaviourist; cognitive and psychodynamic. The question allows you to consider both positive and negative aspects of each model. Here it would be best to choose two contrasting models, for example, the biological model (genetics and biochemical) and a psychological model (behaviourist or psychodynamic).

Question 4

a Choose from the following: abnormality as deviation from social norms; abnormality as statistical infrequency; abnormality as deviation from 'ideal mental health' or abnormality as 'failure to function adequately'. Once you have chosen two definitions you need to provide a detailed account explaining how each account for psychological abnormality. It is also useful to give examples where appropriate.

b One assumption of the medical model is that abnormal behaviour is caused by an underlying physical or organic cause, usually a disfunction of the brain or nervous system. This may be the result of an inherited gene, an imbalance of chemicals in the nervous system and endocrine system or of brain damage. A second assumption concerns the view that abnormal behaviour can be identified and classified in a systematic way. Mental illness is characterised by a particular set of symptoms. A doctor will typically seek to reach a diagnosis by comparing the patient's particular symptoms to those characteristic of various illnesses. Classification systems including DSM-IV allow a doctor to make such diagnoses.

c In considering the implications of the cognitive model for the treatment of abnormal behaviour you need to briefly mention assumptions about the underlying cause. According to the cognitive model, the individual is seen as an active processor of information and it is the way in which individuals perceive, anticipate and evaluate events, rather the events themselves, which have the greatest impact on behaviour. Abnormal behaviour stems from faulty thinking, when thoughts are constantly negative and irrational they may result in maladaptive behaviour. Therefore the aim of therapy is to help the client to identify their negative, irrational thoughts and to replace these with more positive, rational ways of thinking. The therapist encourages the client to become aware of beliefs which contribute to the abnormal behaviour. This often involves direct questioning, such as 'Tell me what you think about …' The therapist does not comment on the irrational or negative nature of these beliefs, instead they are treated as hypotheses and examined for validity. The aim is to help the client better understand where their faulty thinking processes are leading them. It is important to remember that cognitive therapy will only be effective if the cause of the abnormal behaviour stems from faulty thinking.

d You need to consider the extent to which attempts to define psychological abnormality have failed to take into account cultural differences. The issue here concerns the view that what may be considered normal in one culture may not be considered as such in another. Therefore definitions of abnormality, which are by their nature imprecise, are also culturally relative, that is dependent on culture. You need to consider the attempts by psychologists to define psychological abnormality (abnormality as deviation from social norms, abnormality as statistical infrequency, abnormality as deviation from 'ideal mental health' and abnormality as 'failure to function adequately') and identify the problems with these definitions in failing to take into account cultural differences, using examples and research evidence to illustrate your points.

Psychology Specification A

Unit 3: Social Psychology and Research Methods

Time allowed: one hour 15 minutes In Section A, answer ONE question. In Section B, answer ALL questions.	**Information** Mark allocations are indicated in the paper. A maximum of two marks can be awarded for quality of written communication.

Section A: Social Psychology

Answer one question from this Section.
Answer all sections of the question you chose.

  1a Explain, with reference to research in social influence, what is meant by the terms 'experimental validity' and 'ecological validity'. (3 + 3 marks)
    b Describe the aims and conclusions of one research study that has explored obedience to authority. (6 marks)
    c Describe two ethical issues relevant to research in social influence. (3 + 3 marks)
    d *'When people in authority tell us to do something, we tend to follow their orders'*. Evaluate the extent to which psychologists can explain this behaviour. (12 marks)

  2a Describe two reasons why people conform to the majority. (3 + 3 marks)
    b Describe the procedures and findings of one study of minority influence. (6 marks)
    c Describe one explanation of resisting pressures to obey. (6 marks)
    d 'Milgram's experiments undoubtedly helped define many ethical issues and triggered the debate regarding the ethics of research within psychology as a whole' Assess to what extent psychologists have resolved ethical issues in social influence research. (12 marks)

Answers to Section A: Social Psychology

Marking criteria: refer to the tables at the start of this chapter for the precise mark allocations.

Question 1

  a If an experiment has an impact on the participants, forces them to take it seriously and involves them in the procedures then it is said to have experimental validity. The similarity of the laboratory experiment to the events which commonly happen to people in the real world and whether it is possible to generalise from the sample to the target population, is referred to as ecological validity. Answers are likely to refer to the work of Milgram.
  b Appropriate studies include Milgram (1963), Meeus & Raajimakers (1986) and Hofling *et al.* (1966). Note that only the aims and conclusions should be included in the answer.
  c Deception, informed consent and protection of participants are issues relevant to research in social influence. Note that answers should include only two of these.
  d Explanations for obeying include Milgram's agency theory, buffers and gradual commitment. Each explanation included should be briefly described and discussed in terms of its strengths and limitations.

Question 2

    a Answers are likely to include informational and normative influence, Deutch & Gerard (1955). Informational influence is when, in situations when we are uncertain as to how to behave, we look to others to provide information. Normative influence occurs as a result of the need to be accepted and liked, this encourages us to do as other people are doing in order to gain acceptance.

    b Appropriate studies include Clark (1994), a study of minority influence in a jury setting and Moscovici *et al.* (1969), a laboratory study of minority influence involving perception of colour. Note the answer should focus on the procedures and findings only.

    c Answers could refer to previous experience, exposure to disobedient models, education or reactance. Answers are likely to refer to evidence from the variations of Milgram's original procedure.

    d Ethical guidelines concerning issues of deception, informed consent and protection of participants should be included. Debates and empirical evidence concerning these issues should also be outlined, for example, the work of Christensen (1988) and Krupat & Garonzig (1994), indicating that deception in psychological research can sometimes be justified. Issues of debriefing and withdrawal from the investigation could also be included in the discussion.

Section B: Research Methods

Answer ALL questions from this Section.

Question 3

A researcher wished to investigate whether there is a relationship between birth weight and intelligence. A random sample of 20 male participants took part. The researcher tested the participants' intelligence using an IQ test and then asked them for their birth weight. Using these measures, the researcher produced the graph shown in Figure 1.

    a Suggest a suitable non-directional hypothesis for this investigation. (2 marks)

    b Describe one advantage and one weakness of correlational analyses such as these. (2 + 2 marks)

    c Explain what is meant by 'random sampling', and describe how a random sample might have been obtained in this study. (2 + 2 marks)

    d Describe one ethical issue that might have arisen in this study. (2 marks)

    e Name the type of graph shown in Figure 1. (1 mark)

    f Describe the relationship between birth weight and intelligence shown in Figure 1. (2 marks)

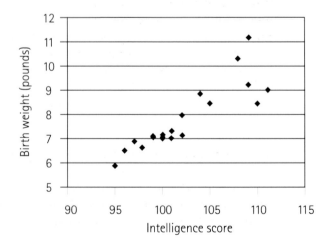

Figure 1 The relationship between birth weight and intelligence

Question 4

Imagine that you wish to investigate the effects of using a mobile phone whilst driving. Your research team decide to use a driving simulator to measure the 'dangerous driving' behaviours of the drivers. The mean number of dangerous driving behaviours per hour will be recorded.

   a Identify two ways in which you could operationalise 'dangerous driving'. (2 marks)
   b Outline the type of experimental design you would use and give one disadvantage of this design. (2 + 2 marks)
   c What would be the independent variable in this investigation? (1 mark)
   d How would you select participants for this study? (2 marks)
   e Why would you choose this particular method of selecting participants? (2 marks)
   f Explain two features of the study that might affect the validity of the data being collected. (2 + 2 marks)

Answers to Section B: Research Methods

Marking criteria: refer to the tables at the start of this chapter for the precise mark allocations.

Question 3

   a 'There will be no (significant) correlation between birth weight and intelligence.'
   b Advantages will include their use where experimental manipulation would be unethical, since they show the relationship between two co-variables they might help to indicate further research topics and can rule out causal relationships. Weaknesses might include the fact they do not establish cause and effect and any relationship may be due to another extraneous variable.
   c Random sampling is where every member of a population has an equal chance of being selected. The easiest way to do this is to draw names (or numbers) from a hat.
   d The use of intelligence scores is controversial and an ethical issue would be whether or not to disclose an individual's result if they asked how they had performed.
   e A scattergram.
   f There is a strong positive correlation. The answer should include both the strength and direction of the correlation.

Question 4

   a When there is little agreement on the best way to measure a concept, operationalisation helps to give a clear and objective definition. Students could identify numerous behaviours which might constitute 'dangerous driving' such as errors concerned with steering, speeding, gear changes, adherence to traffic signs and so on. These could be measured by the number of occurrences or the degree or amount of the error, or possibly a combination of both.
   b Repeated measures, independent measures or matched pair design with an appropriate description. For example, repeated measures design where the same participant is tested in both conditions (using and not using phone). One disadvantage of this design would be order effects, where the participants perform less well in the second condition due to factors such as boredom or fatigue.
   c The independent variable is the use of the phone or not.
   d The most common answer will be random sampling, although quota, stratified or opportunity sampling would be acceptable with an appropriate description.
   e Advantages of the appropriate method chosen need to be given. For example, opportunity sampling would be chosen because it is the easiest and cheapest method in terms of both time and money.
   f These could include demand characteristics, experimenter expectancy effects; ecological validity with an appropriate explanation.